An Atlas of Russian
and East European History

An Atlas of Russian and East European History

Arthur E. Adams, Ian M. Matley,
and William O. McCagg

FREDERICK A. PRAEGER, *Publishers*
New York · Washington

BOOKS THAT MATTER

Published in the United States of America in 1967
by Frederick A. Praeger, Inc., Publishers
111 Fourth Avenue, New York, N.Y. 10003

Library of Congress Catalog Card Number: 66–18884

Printed in the United States of America

Contents

Preface

Our purpose in this atlas has been to present an account in text and maps of the long history of Russia and Eastern Europe. We have attempted to emphasize how this area between Asia and Western Europe shared sometimes in the political and cultural developments of both, suffered often from the depredations of both, yet developed its own distinctive political and cultural forms, which, in turn, significantly influenced both West and East. We believe that the great historical and contemporary importance of this area is too little understood, and it is our hope that the maps drawn here will help make some of the complexities less perplexing and some of the events that at first glance might seem esoteric recognizable as important developments in our world's history and significant for our time.

We wish to thank Donald G. Janelle, our cartographer, for his patient and talented labors upon our maps and Jan Adams for her valuable editorial and typing assistance.

A. E. A.
I. M. M.
W. O. M.

An Atlas of Russian
and East European History

Part I
Basic Data

Because the many national and ethnic boundaries of Russia and Eastern Europe have changed innumerable times in the past, it is impossible to define precisely their principal divisions and subdivisions. But since even imprecise definitions are much more useful than none at all, it is necessary to establish a number of them, more or less arbitrarily, for the purposes of this atlas.

The term *Russia and Eastern Europe* defines the territories within the boundaries of today's Soviet Union and the lands between the Soviet Union's western boundary, the Baltic Sea, the Elbe River, the Adriatic Sea, and the Turkish straits. Russia is commonly divided into *European Russia* (west of the Ural Mountains) and *Asiatic Russia* (from the Urals eastward to the Pacific). In turn, each of these great areas can be subdivided; for example, European Russia is often broken down into Belorussia and the Ukraine, the remainder being considered Russia proper. Similarly, *Eastern Europe* can be segmented. *Northeastern Europe* includes Poland and the Baltic states, East Prussia, and usually other parts of northern Germany; in some definitions, it also includes parts of Scandinavia and northwestern Russia. *Central Europe* includes as its primary areas Bohemia, historic Hungary, and Austria; its peripheries often embrace other German states as well as southern Poland and the western Ukraine. The *Balkans,* of course, can be clearly placed on the Balkan Peninsula, but a glance at the historical maps in this atlas will make it obvious that the northern boundaries have often extended into Central Europe and Russia and that the internal boundaries have constantly shifted.

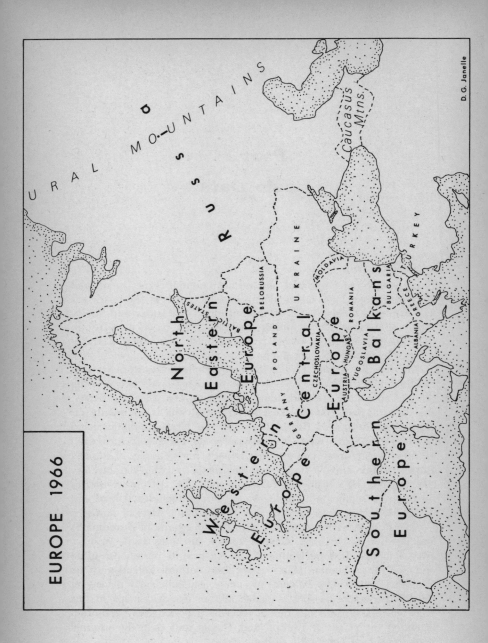

EUROPE 1966

URAL MOUNTAINS

Russia

Caucasus Mtns.

North Eastern Europe

Western Europe

Central Europe

Balkans

Southern Europe

BALTIC STATES

BELORUSSIA

POLAND

UKRAINE

MOLDAVIA

GERMANY

CZECHOSLOVAKIA

AUSTRIA HUNGARY

YUGOSLAVIA

ROMANIA

BULGARIA

ALBANIA GREECE

TURKEY

D.G. Janelle

Geography (Maps 2–4)

The dominant geographical feature of Russia and Eastern Europe is the vast plain stretching from the mountains of eastern Siberia across Eurasia to Germany and the Low Countries, its level expanse broken only by the Ural highlands (*Map 2*). This plain is divided horizontally into three great natural zones, each characterized by distinctive climate, vegetation, and soil (*Map 4*). Along the Arctic coast stretches the tundra—a treeless, forbidding region with little attraction for human settlement. Just south of the tundra lies a great zone of forests—coniferous in the cooler regions of the north and east, deciduous in the warmer, more humid western and southern regions. The third great zone of the Eurasian plain is the grassland, or steppe, extending from Mongolia westward to the Black Sea coast and the lower Danube. In Central Asia the steppe, particularly in its southern reaches, is arid and even desert, but at its western end it has adequate precipitation for agriculture and forms an attractive area for rural settlement.

The Eurasian plain is broken by many rivers (*Maps 2, 3*). Some of the greatest of these are in Siberia, where the Lena, Enisei, and Ob flow into the Arctic Ocean. But these Siberian rivers have been relatively useless to man because they are icebound much of the year and are of little value as transportation routes between east and west. Correspondingly, the river systems of central Asia have been of little use, since they either evaporate in the desert or flow into the landlocked Aral Sea. At the European end of the vast plain, however, the rivers are of a beneficial character. The mighty Volga, although it flows into the landlocked Caspian, serves as a natural pathway from Iran and the east deep into the northern Russian woodlands. Its headwaters are only a short portage from those of the Dvina, which empties into the Baltic, and from the Dnepr, which ends in the Black Sea. The portage is also short between the Volga and the Don at their great bends, affording easy passage from the Volga to the Sea of Azov and the Black Sea. The two major tributaries of the Volga, the Oka and the Kama, provide a continuous water route from south of Moscow to the Urals. Farther west, there are natural pathways between the Dnestr, flowing into the Black Sea, and the valleys of the Vistula, the Oder, and the Elbe, which drain into the Baltic.

Along the southern edge of the plain lie complex systems of

mountain ranges (*Maps 2, 3*). Stretching westward from the mountain systems of eastern Siberia are the Altai Mountains and the Tien Shan of Central Asia, then the Afghan and Iranian ranges (the Pamirs and the Hindu Kush), the peaks of the Caucasus, the rugged Balkans, and the long line of the Carpathians, ending in Bohemia across the Danube from the Alps. These ranges constitute a great barrier separating northern Eurasia from the south. In Asia, there are several paths through this barrier. The Jungarian Gap serves as a road between China and Kazakhstan, as the Khyber Pass does between Central Asia and India. Perhaps the most inviting breaks in the great succession of mountains, however, are at the southwestern ends of the plain, where the Black Sea offers an open waterway into the warm Mediterranean and where the Danube acts as an invitation into the Mid-Danube Plain, with its narrow but easy accesses to the Aegean, the Adriatic, and Western Europe.

At the southwestern end of the plain, in Southeastern Europe, the mountains tend to encircle and protect rather than to isolate the lowlands (*Map 3*). In the shadow of the Carpathians lie the Bohemian Highland, the Pannonian Plains, and Transylvania, all offering favorable conditions for settled agriculture.

The vast plain that dominates Russia and Eastern Europe has significantly influenced the course of the area's history. The steppe, in particular, has acted as a natural highway along which the nomad tribes of Mongolia and Siberia have traveled westward. When the nomads could penetrate southward into India and the Middle East, the temptation to move west was not great. But when, as often happened, entry into the Asiatic South was blocked by great empires, the easy steppe route and the attractions of Mediterranean civilization acted as magnets for westward movement (*Maps 8, 10, 11, 13, 18*). The encouragement of westward-moving nomads has been only one of the plain's influences. Since time immemorial, the river systems in the western regions of the great plain have inspired movement of peoples and trade from Scandinavia and the Baltic to the Black Sea, the Aegean, and the East (*Maps 11, 13*).

The Balkan and Carpathian mountains have influenced history by acting as effective obstacles to major extensions of Near Eastern civilization into Northeastern Europe and the steppe. It was the Danube, not the Dnepr or the Volga, that formed the frontier of the Roman Empire (*Map 8*). Most of Central and Northeastern Europe was settled, not from the civilized South, but by Slavs and Germans moving eastward along the great plain from their Baltic homelands (*Maps 8, 9, 16*).

Russia, which eventually received its culture from the Near East, was later cut off and isolated from that source for centuries by nomad movements on the steppe (*Maps 12, 13*). And, although the Ottoman Empire extended its authority beyond the Danube to the mouths of the Dnepr and the Volga, it was never able to control the steppe (*Maps 21, 24, 34*).

IA—PHYSICAL

Laptev
Sea

Anadyr
Plateau

Chersky Range

Verkhoyansk Range

Central

Siberian

Plateau

Nizhne Tunguska

Lena Rr.

Angara R.

L.
Baikal

Sea of
Okhotsk

Great Khingan Range

Amur Rr.

Sikhote-Alin

Gobi   Desert

| 0 | 500 | 1000 |

M I L E S

DGJ

Over 10,000 ft.

Over 3,000 ft.

Over 600 ft.

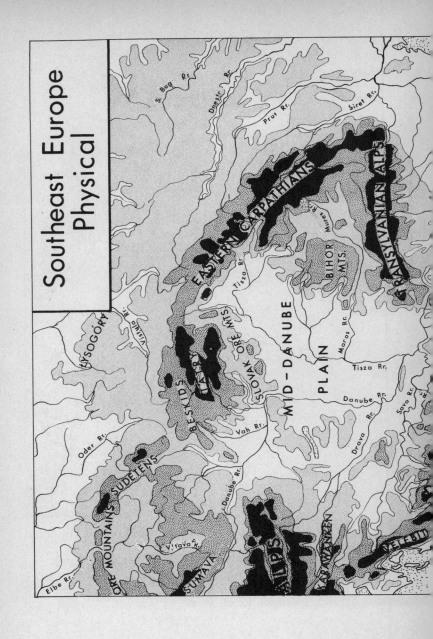

Southeast Europe
Physical

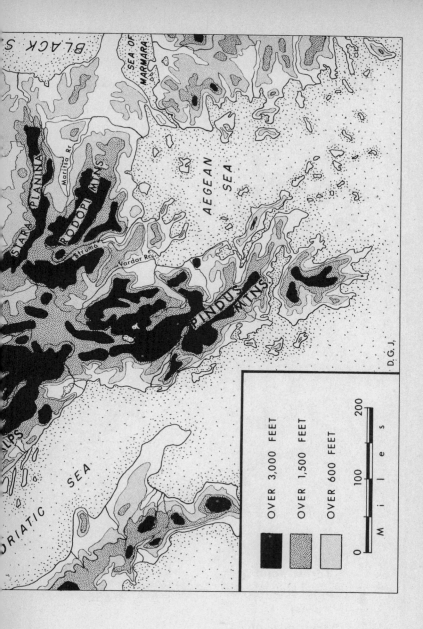

BLACK S

SEA OF MARMARA

STARA PLANINA

Maritsa R.

RODOPI MTNS.

Struma

Vardar R.

PINDUS MTNS.

AEGEAN SEA

ALPS

ADRIATIC SEA

D.G.J.

OVER 3,000 FEET

OVER 1,500 FEET

OVER 600 FEET

M i l e s

0   100   200

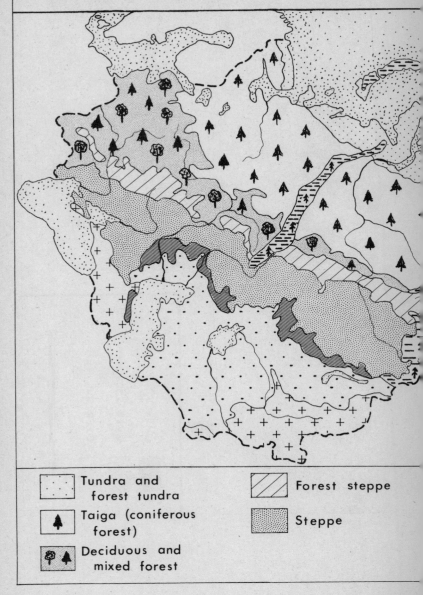

NATURAL REGIONS OF THE SOVIET U

Tundra and forest tundra

Taiga (coniferous forest)

Deciduous and mixed forest

Forest steppe

Steppe

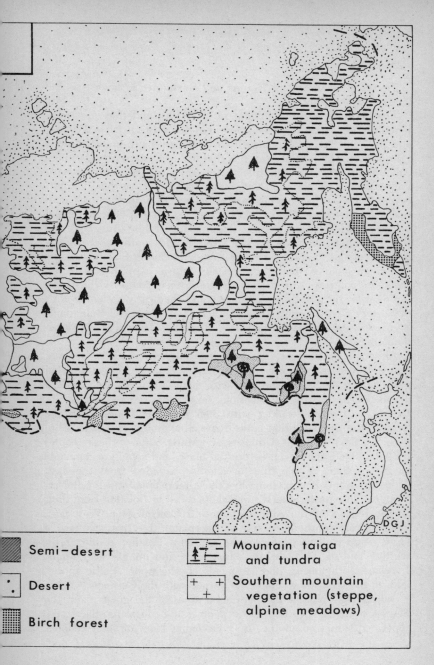

	Semi-desert		Mountain taiga and tundra
	Desert		Southern mountain vegetation (steppe, alpine meadows)
	Birch forest		

DGJ

13

Peoples (MAPS 5, 6)

The peoples of Eastern Europe and Russia are as diverse as the lands in which they live.

The Slavs form the dominant racial group, and they are traditionally classified into three branches—the Eastern, the Western, and the Southern, each of which encompasses many smaller groups (*Maps 5, 6*). The largest branch is that of the Eastern Slavs, usually called the Russians; within this branch, the Great Russians are most important, for they occupy the greater part of the northeastern forest lands of Europe, having extended their territories in past centuries by colonizing Siberia (*Map 6; see also 41, 44*). Closely related to the Great Russians are the Belorussians (White Russians) and the Ukrainians, who inhabit the western and southwestern areas, respectively, of the present Soviet Union. The other Slavic branches are much smaller than the Russians and occupy far more restricted territories (*Map 6*). The Western Slavs comprise the Poles, the Slovaks, the Czechs (Bohemians), and the nearly extinct Wends of Eastern German lands. The Southern Slavs comprise Bulgarians, Serbs, Croats, Slovenes, and the ethnically less distinct Macedonians.

Although the Czechs, Slovaks, and Southern Slavs are mountain dwellers, the majority of the Slavs inhabit the great Russian plain, where they share the land with many other peoples (*Map 5*). To the north, on the tundra, small groups of Nentsy (Samoedes), Evenki, and others wander with their herds of reindeer. In the heart of the Great Russian lands live sizable groups of Tatars, Chuvash, Bashkirs, Mordvas, Udmurts, and Maris. Some of these peoples probably lived there even before the Slavs, and some are remnants of groups that, at one time or another, invaded from the east. Along the frontier with China live the Altai peoples and the Buriat-Mongols; in eastern Siberia, the Iakuts dwell in isolation from their Turkic fellows of the Altai plateau and Central Asia. Westward, along a vast southern stretch of the plain, the Russians face a large group of Turkic people, the Kazakhs. Finally, at the northwestern end of the plain, the Slavs meet and mingle with Finns, Latvians, Lithuanians, and Estonians on the upper Baltic shores, and, to the west, they stand face to face with the Germans.

Where they inhabit the peripheral areas of the great plain, the Slavs are mixed with non-Slavic peoples and, in some places, are separated from one another by intervening blocs of such peoples.

In the mountains around Bohemia (the Sudetenland), in the mining areas of Slovakia and Transylvania, and in the rich agricultural lands bounded by the Danube, the Eastern Carpathians, and the Transylvanian Alps, the Slavs dwelt, until recently, side by side with Germans (*Maps 3, 6*). Along the Danube, in a broad belt running from the Black Sea to German Austria, dwell the considerable non-Slavic blocs—the Romanians (Vlachs) and Hungarians (Magyars). In the eastern and southern Balkans, large tracts of territory are inhabited jointly by Albanians, Greeks, Turks, and Slavs (*Map 6*). At the eastern end of the Black Sea, in the Caucasus, Slavs dwell in inseparably entangled communities with Georgians, Armenians, and Azerbaijanians (*Map 5*).

As if to add to the complexity of the enthnography of Russia and Eastern Europe, the different branches of the Slavic family are themselves inextricably—often unhappily—intermixed. This is particularly true on the borderlands of the Western and Eastern Slavs, (i.e., in Poland and the western Ukraine), in Bosnia-Herzegovina, and in Macedonia (*Map 6*).

The complicated intermixture of the peoples of Eastern Europe and Russia has been partially altered by massive population movements in the twentieth century. Of these, one of the most notable was the final evacuation of the Turks from the Balkan lands they once ruled. Begun in the nineteenth century, this movement was furthered by the formal Greco-Turkish population exchange in the 1920's and was virtually completed by the evacuation of the "Pomaks" (Bulgarian-speaking Moslems) from Bulgaria after World War II (*Map 87*). A second great population change of the twentieth century resulted from the systematic slaughter of Jews by the Germans during the 1940's, which virtually annihilated the Jewish communities of Poland and the Ukraine (*Map 65*). A third significant change occurred after World War II, when Czechoslovakia and Poland, with the encouragement of the Allies, expelled the German-speaking populations from their ancient homes in the Sudetenland, Prussia, Pomerania, and Silesia. Other less extensive expulsions of Germans took place in 1945 and thereafter in Transylvania, Yugoslavia, and Hungary. Also in 1945, there was a movement of Poles into lands taken from the Germans and a population exchange between Czechoslovakia and Hungary (*Maps 86, 88, 90*). A final major category of population movements in this century was Stalin's virtual extermination, during World War II, of several Soviet nationality groups and the extensive deportations involved in the Sovietization of the Baltic area and what was once eastern Poland.

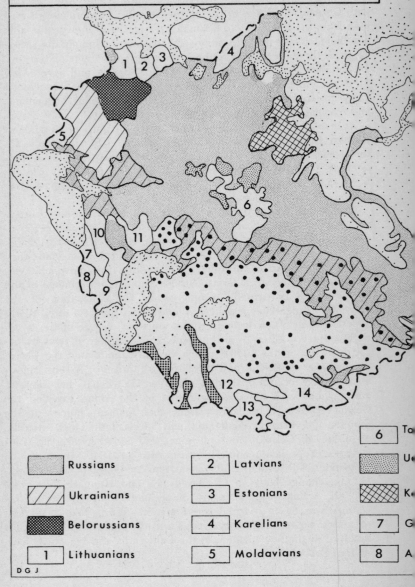

PEOPLES OF THE SOVIET UNION

Russians

Ukrainians

Belorussians

1 Lithuanians

2 Latvians

3 Estonians

4 Karelians

5 Moldavians

6 Ta

U

Ke

7 G

8 A

DGJ

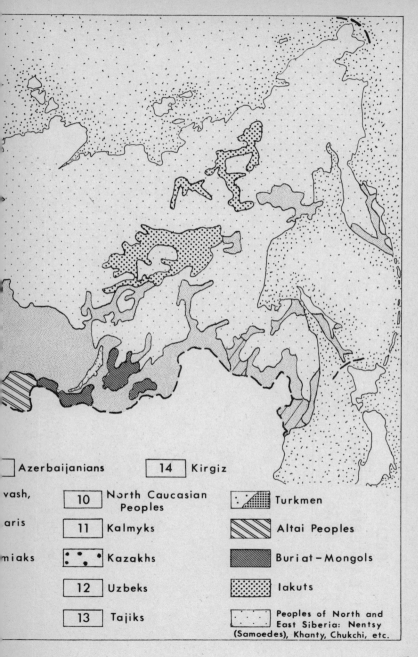

Azerbaijanians	14 Kirgiz		
vash,	10 North Caucasian Peoples	Turkmen	
aris	11 Kalmyks	Altai Peoples	
miaks	Kazakhs	Buriat–Mongols	
	12 Uzbeks	Iakuts	
	13 Tajiks	Peoples of North and East Siberia: Nentsy (Samoedes), Khanty, Chukchi, etc.	

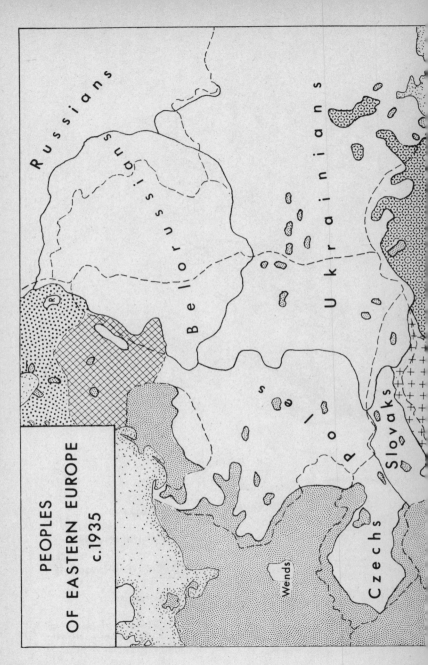

PEOPLES
OF EASTERN EUROPE
c.1935

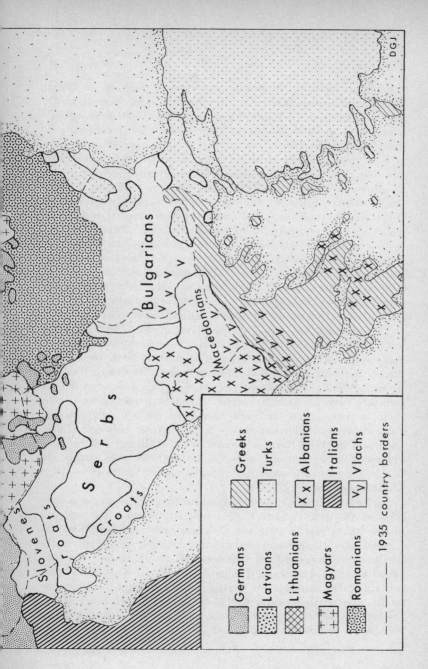

Slovenes

Croats

Croats

Serbs

Bulgarians

v v v

Macedonians

v

v v v

x x x

x x x x

x x x x

x x x x x x

x x v x

x x x x v v x x

x x x v v x

v v v

v

v v v

x x x

x x x

x

x x x x

x x x

x

DGJ

Germans		Greeks
Latvians		Turks
Lithuanians		Albanians
Magyars		Italians
Romanians		Vlachs

————— 1935 country borders

19

Religions (MAP 7)

Religious diversity is also a characteristic feature of Eastern Europe and Russia (*Map* 7). The Russians have long been Orthodox Christians. In Central Asia, they have coexisted with Islamic peoples, while, in eastern Siberia, they are contiguous with Buddhist peoples (*Map 5*). In neither of these cases is there a history of great religious conflict. Within the Orthodox community, however, there has been a record of persecutions of sectarians since the fifteenth century and of the "Old Believers," who split from the official church in the seventeenth century. Furthermore, although Orthodoxy has allowed Protestant communities to exist in its midst, it has systematically persecuted Catholics and the huge Jewish community absorbed by Russia in the eighteenth century (*Maps 40, 65*). In the mountainous areas of the Caucasus, Orthodox Russians live alongside Moslem Azerbaijanians and autocephalous Christian communities of Georgians and Armenians, peoples who have fought holy wars against one another for centuries.

In Eastern Europe, there exist religious frontiers between Islam and Christianity, as well as barriers among the Christians themselves (*Map 7*). As in the Caucasus, these frontiers coincide in many cases with ethnic frontiers and have led to bitter conflicts. In the north, the Roman Catholic Poles live next to Orthodox Russians. In both Polish and Russian eyes, this religious difference has for centuries been as great a barrier to peaceful intercourse as any chain of high mountains could have been (*Map 7; see also 40*). Poland's western boundary is a religious frontier between Catholicism and northern German Protestantism. Although this religious difference has existed only since the sixteenth century, it adds fuel to the German-Slavic nationality conflict, which is almost as old as Christianity (*Maps 7, 15*).

In Central Europe, serious divisions among Christians have complicated the region's history. One religious frontier, for example, divides the Catholic southern Germans and Austrians from the Czechs, who, though nominally Catholic today, developed in the late medieval period a Protestant national cult (Hussitism) and have preserved its traditions. In Hungarian history, German Catholicism is traditionally counterposed to Hungarian Calvinism. Furthermore, in the nineteenth century, Catholics among the Hungarians oppressed the Lutherans among the Slovaks, as well as the Orthodox Romanians and Serbs (*Map 7; see also 32, 48*). For several centuries, in Transylvania and in Southern Poland, the religious heterogeneity was compounded by the presence of a sizable body of Orthodox Christians, the Uniates, who were in more or less unwilling communion with the Roman Church (*Map 7; see also 86, 98*). After World War II, the bulk of these were forcibly returned to Russian Orthodoxy.

In the Balkans, if ethnic conflicts do not set one group against another, religious diversity does. The Serbs and Croats, ethnically almost identical, are divided into hostile Orthodox and Catholic communities (*Maps 7, 10*). The Bulgarians and Slovenes are similarly divided. Yet, the Catholic Slovenes and Croats, on the one hand, and the Orthodox Serbs and Bulgarians, on the other, do not see eye to eye. In the latter case, especially, the reverse is true—the Serbs have bitterly fought the Bulgarians (*Map 7; see also 63, 77, 91*). Furthermore, there is little unity among the Orthodox Greeks, Serbs, and Bulgarians, the Greeks having for many centuries attempted to eliminate the autonomy of the Serbian and Bulgarian branches of Orthodoxy. The Albanians are divided among Islam, Orthodoxy, and Catholicism, and each group has habitually fought with the others. The signal importance of religion in the Balkans is perhaps best illustrated by an aspect of the Greco-Turkish population exchange that followed World War I. Turkish-speaking Christians, who had lived for centuries in Anatolia, were "repatriated" to Greece, and Greek-speaking Moslems, who had always lived on the island of Crete, were "repatriated" to Turkey (*Map 7; see also 87*).

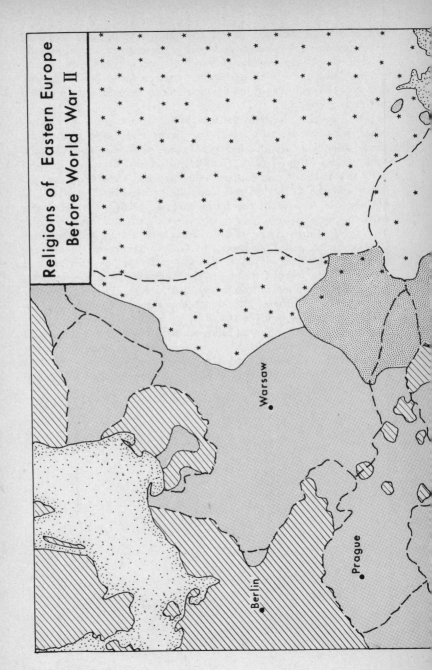

Religions of Eastern Europe
Before World War II

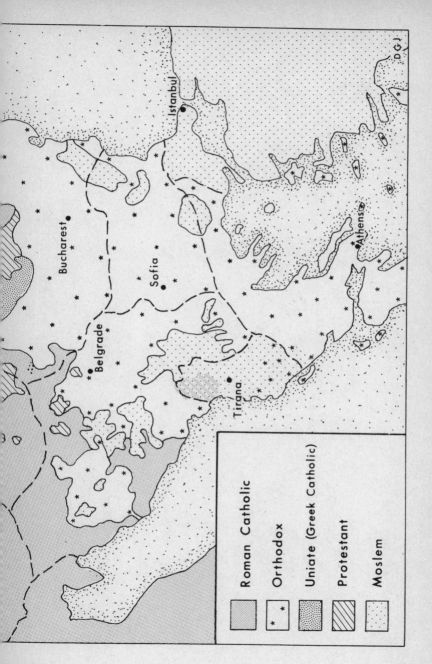

Roman Catholic

Orthodox

Uniate (Greek Catholic)

Protestant

Moslem

Istanbul

Bucharest

Belgrade

Sofia

Tirana

Athens

D.G.J.

23

Part II
Eastern Europe and Russia
Prior to 1530

Western Europe was already a community of sorts in Roman times. Eastern Europe and Russia formed no comparable community. After the fall of Rome in 410 A.D., Western Europe, as a community, witnessed first a weakening of civilizing influences, then a revival of learning. Accordingly, one can refer to "ancient," "medieval," and "modern" periods in Western European history. Eastern Europe and Russia saw no such sequence of fall and rise. The Balkans stood within the orbit of a seat of learning, Greece, that flourished continuously from before the foundation of Rome until a thousand years after the sacking of Rome by the barbarians. Northeastern Europe and Russia were tribal lands until after 1000 A.D. (*Map* 8). Therefore, to speak of a "medieval" period in the history of the eastern regions would erroneously imply that Byzantine civilization was no more than a remnant of the Latin past and that a significant "ancient" culture existed in the forests north of Rome's frontier. In a history of Eastern Europe and Russia, the terms "ancient" and "medieval" can only define chronological periods of time.

Even in reference to the sixteenth century, one can speak of a community of the lands of Eastern Europe and Russia only with hesitation. To contemporaries, the contrasts between Poland, Hungary, Bohemia, the eastern German lands, the Balkans, and Russia probably seemed far more striking than the similarities. Particularism was universal, for these nations had traveled a variety of political roads during the previous millennium. Also, this was a religious age. In these lands dwelt followers of Roman Catholicism, Greek and Russian Orthodoxy, Protestantism, Judaism, and Islam. The few educated inhabitants of the area spoke Latin, Greek, one of the Slavic tongues, or Arabic. These differences emphasized diversity rather than unity.

Yet, despite this diversity, by 1530, men could see that the greatest of the old divisions within Eastern Europe, the contrast between the barbarian Eurasian plain and the civilized Balkan littoral, had disappeared. On the one hand, Germanic and Slavic tribesmen had settled down and had accepted Christianity and European or Byzantine social forms (*Maps 9–13, 16, 22*). On the other hand, Gothic, Hunnish, Bulgar, and Magyar invasions had ruined the provinces of the Byzantine Empire: by 1453, a Moslem master had ravished its core, Constantinople, and had reduced the peoples of the Balkans to a state far more humble than that of the one-time barbarians to the north (*Maps 8, 10, 17, 21, 24*). Moreover, men of the 1530's could see that the barrier between Eastern Europe and Russia was breaking down (*See maps 36, 37*). In 1533, Ivan the Terrible ascended the Muscovite throne and formally claimed the succession of Imperial Rome and Byzantium for Moscow, "the third Rome." Ivan's reign marked the decisive entry of Russia into European politics. Finally, by the 1530's, contemporaries could see that the Christian lands between the Elbe and the Urals faced a common enemy (*Maps 33, 34*). Just prior to 1500, the Ottoman Turks won suzerainty over the Tatar khanates along the northern littoral of the Black Sea. In 1526, the Ottomans conquered Hungary. In 1529, they besieged Vienna. The peoples of Central Europe and Russia could recognize that unless they devised effective measures of self-defense, they might all share the fate of the Christian Balkans.

Still other factors bound the lands of Eastern Europe and Russia into a semblance of a community in the 1530's. Greatest of these were the introduction of serfdom and a growing economic and cultural subordination to the West (*Map 28*). Contemporaries did not have the historical perspective to understand the significance of such developments; yet the latter were as important as Christianity in helping to create cultural and institutional similarities among the lands of Eastern Europe and Russia.

Christianization and the New Polities (MAPS 8–13)

The first step in the emergence of the community of Eastern Europe and Russia was the extension of Hellenic and, later, Christian influences into the forests and steppes of Eurasia.

Of the spread of Hellenic culture, little is known. Greek sources say that Hellenic traders settled the northern shores of the Black Sea and penetrated to the coast of the Baltic. These sources leave unclear, however, such matters as the original homelands of the Slavs (*Map 8*).

The spread of Christianity in Northeastern Europe was sporadic until the days of Charlemagne. It probably began even before the official conversion of the Roman Empire to Christianity in the fourth century. When, in the fourth century, the Huns fled their Asiatic pastures and drove the Germanic peoples (the Visigoths, Vandals, Ostrogoths, Burgundians, and Franks) of the western steppe to seek refuge within the Empire, some of the latter had already accepted the doctrines of the Christian heretic Arius. Subsequently, between the sixth and eighth centuries, Christianity ebbed in Eastern Europe. In this period, the pagan Avars held sway in Pannonia, the Moslem Arabs laid waste the shores of Greece, and one of the three great Slavic groups, the Southern, crossed the Carpathians and the Danube, dechristianizing the Balkans.

With Charlemagne (768–814), Christianity made its definitive entry into Eastern Europe (*Map 9*). One of the reasons for this was probably the end of the Arab threat, which, in the preceding age, had distracted Christian centers from missionary activity. In the West, Charles Martel repulsed the Moslem vanguard at Tours in 732; in the East, the Byzantine Emperor Leo preserved Constantinople from the Arabs' siege in 718. A new wave of Christianization was also made possible when Charlemagne defeated the Avars in the Mid-Danube Plain, conquered the Elbian Saxons, and thus opened the entire East to Frankish missionaries (*Map 9*). A third reason for the new Christianization was that, because of Charlemagne, Christianity acquired special attractions for the pagan tribes of the East. Through collaboration with the papacy, Charlemagne won an imperial title for himself. Other pagan tribes, threatened by his might, saw that they could gain through emulation of his example.

After Charlemagne, the Christianization of Eastern Europe took another two centuries to complete (*Maps 10, 12*). In the middle of the ninth century, the Slavic rulers of Moravia invited Greek missionaries to bring them the benefits of Christianity without the inconvenience of Frankish suzerainty. About the same time, the Bulgars extended a similar bid for a Latin mission so they might become Christian without suffering Greek dominion. In 1924, the Croats tried to escape both Frankish and Greek overlordship by obtaining a royal crown directly from the pope; the crown symbolized Rome's patronage of Croatian independence. These attempts at political independence failed when Magyar tribes fled the steppe (about 900) because of attacks by the Asiatic Patzinacs (Pechenegs). Forced westward, the Magyars invaded Pannonia, beat back Bulgaria, and overran Croatia (*Maps 10, 11*). But the expansion of Christianity did not end. A century later, the Magyars accepted the faith after defeat by the German Emperor Otto I and the offer of a symbolic crown by Rome (*Map 12*). Around the same time, the chieftains of the Slavic Poles turned to Roman Christianity in order to escape German political pressures.

Meanwhile, Byzantium also won converts. In 1014, Basil II defeated the Bulgarian Empire, making possible the extension of direct Greek religious influence throughout the Balkans. In the ninth century, Varangian (Scandinavian) traders established the first Russian polity, Kievan Rus (*Map 11*), and in the tenth century, this new state accepted the Greek faith (*Map 13*). Russia's acceptance of Orthodox Christianity established a strong obstacle to the development of Slavic cultural unity and set the stage for centuries of bitter conflict with the Latin Christian states of Europe. Nonetheless, this act marked an addition to Christianity far larger than the more famous gains of the Latin crusaders in the Holy Land a century later (*Map 15*).

In 1024, when the Poles received their crown from Rome, the Christianization of Northeastern Europe was far from complete. The southern shore of the Baltic was still pagan and would remain so until the colonizing crusades of the Germans in the twelfth and thirteenth centuries (*Maps 12, 16*). The lower Danube and the Black Sea steppe also remained pagan, and the freshly converted Slavic and Magyar lands had only a veneer of "civilization." Nevertheless, the first stage in the formation of a community in Eastern Europe and Russia was well along.

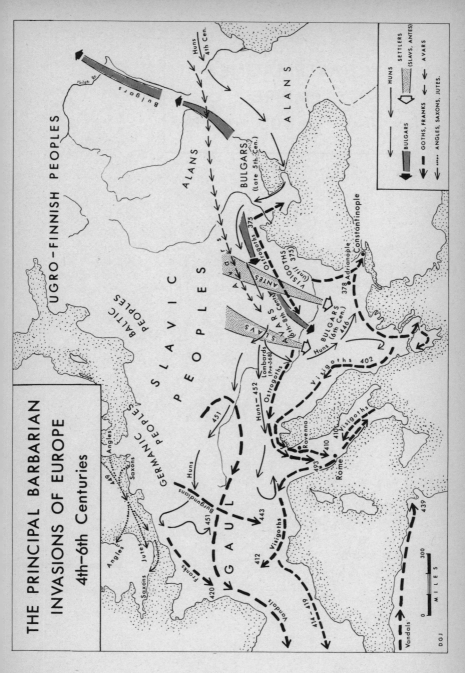

THE PRINCIPAL BARBARIAN
INVASIONS OF EUROPE
4th–6th Centuries

UGRO-FINNISH PEOPLES

BALTIC
PEOPLES

GERMANIC PEOPLES

Angles
Saxons
Angles
Jutes
Saxons
Franks

SLAVIC

PEOPLES

ALANS

ALANS

ALANS

Bulgars

Volga R.

Huns 4th Cen.

BULGARS
(late 5th Cen.)

Ostrogoths 375

VISIGOTHS (until) 375

ANTES (Slavs)

AVARS (6th–8th Cen.)

SLAVS

BULGARS
(6th Cen.)

Huns

378 Adrianople

Constantinople

Visigoths 402

Visigoths 446

Ravenna

410 Visigoths

493

Rome 410

Huns—452

Ostrogoths

Lombards
(Pre-568)

Huns 451

451

Huns
451

Burgundians

G A U L

443

Visigoths

412

Vandals

414–419

420

Franks

Vandals 439

SETTLERS
(SLAVS, ANTES)

HUNS
BULGARS
GOTHS, FRANKS
ANGLES, SAXONS, JUTES.
AVARS

0   300
MILES

MAP 8   /29

D.G.J.

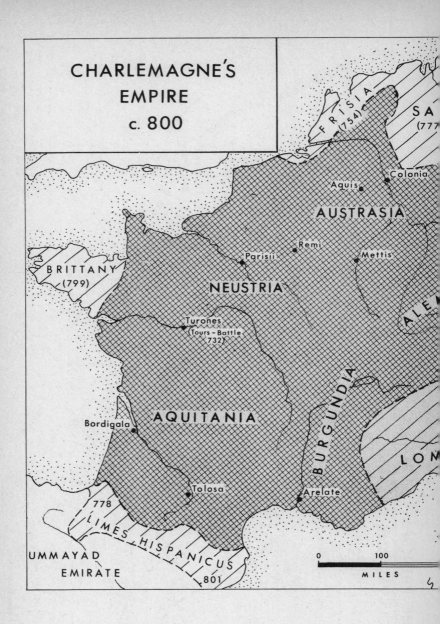

CHARLEMAGNE'S
EMPIRE
c. 800

FRISIA
(754)

SA
(777

Colonia

Aquis

AUSTRASIA

Remi

Parisii

Mettis

BRITTANY
(799)

NEUSTRIA

ALE

Turones
(Tours–Battle
732)

AQUITANIA

BURGUNDIA

Bordigala

LO

Tolosa

Arelate

778

LIMES HISPANICUS

801

UMMAYAD
EMIRATE

0   100

MILES

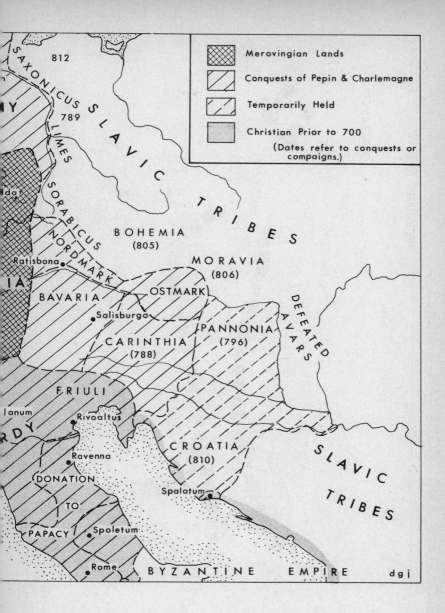

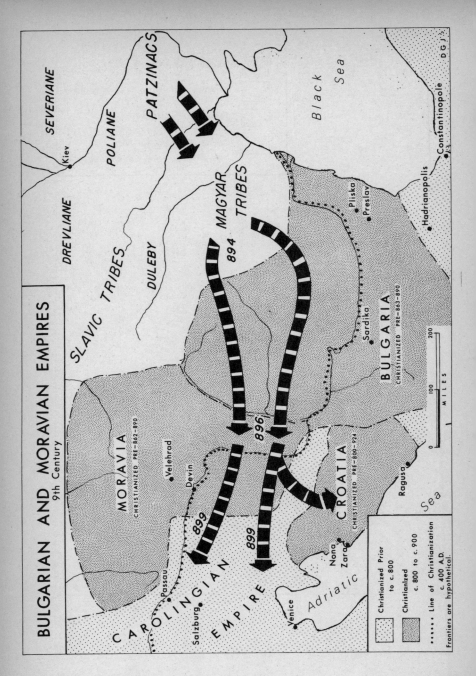

BULGARIAN AND MORAVIAN EMPIRES
9th Century

SEVERIANE
POLIANE
PATZINACS
Kiev
DREVLIANE
DULEBY
SLAVIC TRIBES
MAGYAR TRIBES
894
896
899
899

Black Sea

Constantinopole
Hadrianopolis
Pliska
Preslav
Sardika

BULGARIA
CHRISTIANIZED PRE–863–890

MORAVIA
CHRISTIANIZED PRE–863–890
Velehrad
Devin
Passau
Salzburg

CAROLINGIAN EMPIRE

CROATIA
CHRISTIANIZED PRE–800–924
Ragusa
Nona
Zara
Venice
Adriatic Sea

200
100
0
MILES

Christianized Prior to c. 800
Christianized c. 800 to c. 900
Line of Christianization c. 400 A.D.
Frontiers are hypothetical.

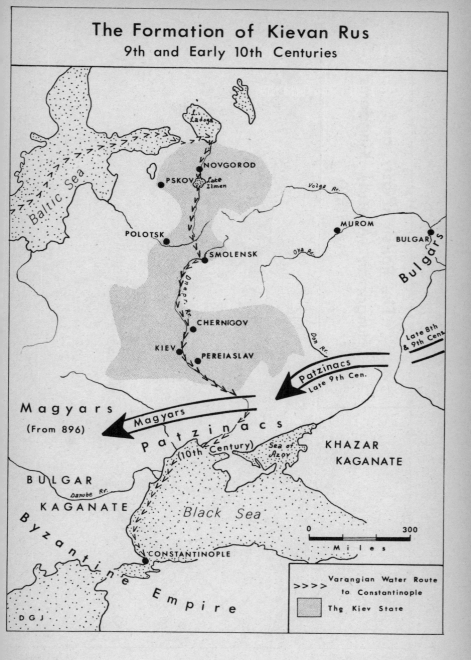

The Formation of Kievan Rus
9th and Early 10th Centuries

Baltic Sea

L. Ladoga

NOVGOROD

PSKOV

Lake Ilmen

Volga Rr.

POLOTSK

MUROM

BULGAR

Bulgars

SMOLENSK

Oka Rr.

Dnepr Rr.

Don Rr.

CHERNIGOV

KIEV

PEREIASLAV

Late 8th & 9th Cent.

Patzinacs
Late 9th Cen.

Magyars

(From 896)

Magyars

Patzinacs

(10th Century)

Sea of Azov

KHAZAR KAGANATE

BULGAR

Danube Rr.

KAGANATE

Black Sea

0   300
Miles

Byzantine Empire

CONSTANTINOPLE

>>>> Varangian Water Route to Constantinople

The Kiev State

D G J

MAP 11   / 33

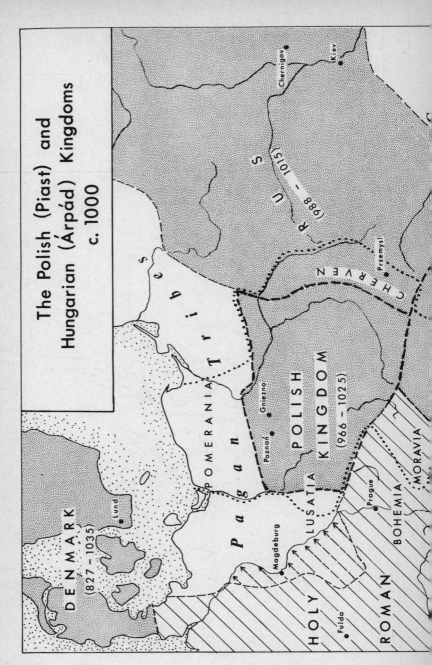

The Polish (Piast) and Hungarian (Árpád) Kingdoms c. 1000

DENMARK
(827 – 1035)

Lund

P a g a n

P o m e r a n i a   T r i b e s

Gniezno

Poznań

POLISH

KINGDOM

(966 – 1025)

LUSATIA

Magdeburg

Prague

BOHEMIA

MORAVIA

HOLY

ROMAN

Fulda

CHERVEN

Przemysl

R (988 – 1015)

U S

Chernigov

Kiev

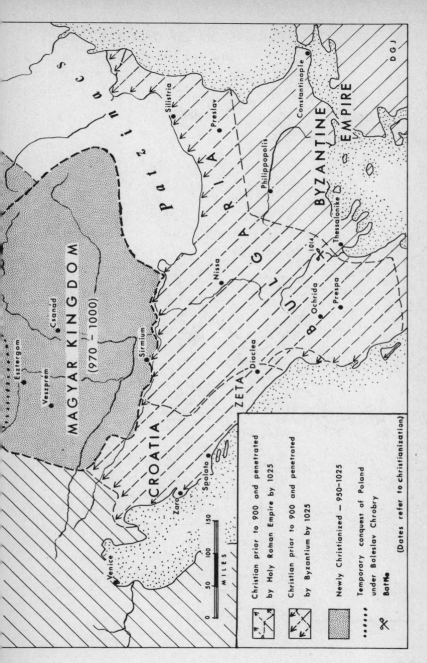

MAGYAR KINGDOM
(970 – 1000)

BYZANTINE EMPIRE

BULGARIA

CROATIA

ZETA

Patzinacs

Esztergom
Veszprem
Csanad
Sirmium
Spalato
Zara
Venice
Dioclea
Nissa
Ochrida
Prespa
Thessalonike
Philippopolis
Silistria
Preslav
Constantinople

1014

Christian prior to 900 and penetrated
by Holy Roman Empire by 1025

Christian prior to 900 and penetrated
by Byzantium by 1025

Newly Christianized — 950–1025

Temporary conquest of Poland
under Boleslav Chrobry

Battle

(Dates refer to christianization)

MILES
0   50   100   150

35

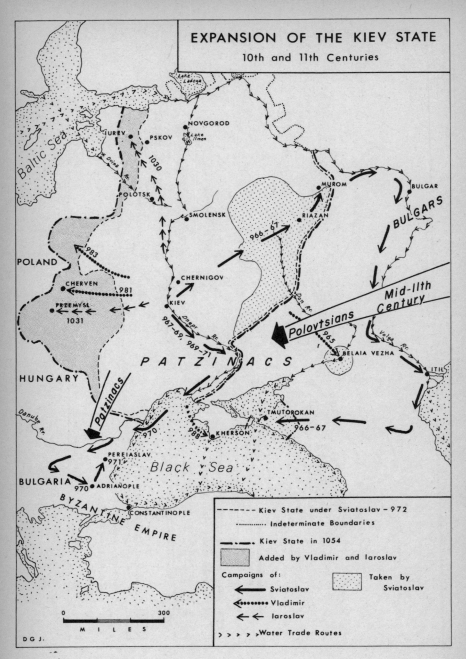

EXPANSION OF THE KIEV STATE
10th and 11th Centuries

Baltic Sea

POLAND

HUNGARY

Lake Ladoga

IUREV
PSKOV
NOVGOROD
Lake Ilmen

1030

POLOTSK

SMOLENSK

981

CHERVEN

981

PRZEMYSL
1031

CHERNIGOV

KIEV

967-69, 969-71

P A T Z I N A C S

Danube Rr.

Patzinacs

970

988

KHERSON

PEREIASLAV
971

BULGARIA

970 ADRIANOPLE

Black Sea

BYZANTINE
EMPIRE

CONSTANTINOPLE

MUROM

RIAZAN

966-67

BULGAR

BULGARS

Mid-11th Century

Polovtsians

965

BELAIA VEZHA

Volga Rr.

ITIL

TMUTOROKAN

966-67

Don Rr.

Dnepr Rr.

W. Dvina Rr.

_ _ _ _ _ Kiev State under Sviatoslav—972
· · · · · · · Indeterminate Boundaries
— · — · — Kiev State in 1054
░░░░ Added by Vladimir and Iaroslav

Campaigns of:

◄━━━ Sviatoslav
◄••••• Vladimir
◄━ ◄━ Iaroslav
> > > > Water Trade Routes

Taken by Sviatoslav

0   300
M I L E S

D G J.

36 /   MAP 13

Thirteenth-Century Catastrophes and Their Political Consequences (MAPS 14–26)

Two great catastrophes strongly influenced the development of Eastern Europe and Russia during the centuries after the introduction of Christianity. In 1204, Latin crusaders sacked Constantinople. And in 1236–42, Mongol, or, as the Russians called them, "Tatar," invaders conquered the lands of Russia and laid waste Hungary, Poland, and Bulgaria (*Maps 18, 19*).

The crusaders' onslaught climaxed a long decline in Byzantine power. In 1071, the Seljuk Turks had defeated Byzantine forces at Mantzikert in Armenia and, thereafter, had overrun Asia Minor (*Map 15*). In the same year, Norman adventurers had seized Byzantium's possessions in southern Italy and had then attacked the Balkan Peninsula. Their attack was followed, after 1095, by the disruptive incursion of crusader armies on their way to the Holy Land. During the twelfth century, Byzantium was so weakened that the emperors were compelled to grant extraordinary commercial privileges to the Venetians in return for naval support; then they were forced to make further concessions to other Italian merchants in order to weaken the Venetian monopoly. Despite these successive misfortunes, until the early thirteenth century, East Rome remained what it had been for centuries—the major centripetal force in the Near East. This the Latin crusaders shattered in 1204.

The result was a void of authority in which anarchic forces multiplied (*Map 17*). The crusaders founded an "empire" at Constantinople. The Greeks clustered around rival poles at Nicaea and Epirus. Feudal dynasties arose in Bulgaria and Serbia. But in the wars that ensued no power was able to establish its ascendancy for long. During the 1230's, it seemed as if Bulgaria might re-establish central authority, but the Tatars, who ravished Bulgaria in 1242 and defeated the Seljuk Turks two years later, inadvertently enabled the Nicaean Greeks to seize the prize (*Maps 17, 18*). Divided among themselves, however, the Greeks lapsed into civil war. Consequently, even mountainous Serbia was able to assemble sufficient strength to make a significant bid for power under Tsar Dušan (1331–55). In the end, the true victors of 1204, apart from the Venetians, were not the polities that fought over the spoils, but the migrant Ottoman Turks and the long-submerged Albanian and Vlach pastoral tribes (*Map 21*). The former entered the Balkans in 1345 by invitation of the warring Greeks, and the latter, taking advantage of the absence of established authority, wandered freely from their highlands to new homes. In later years, the Turks defeated the Serbs and Bulgarians at the Battle of Kosovo Polje (1389), captured Constantinople (1453), and subjected the Balkans to their rule (*Map 21*).

* * * * *

In Northeastern Europe and Russia, as in the Balkans, the thirteenth-century catastrophes struck after a long period of debilitating change. The chieftains who accepted Christianity for Bohemia, Hungary, Poland, and Kievan Rus had established governments that rested, in general, on informal rotation of leadership according to seniority within the ruling family. When the tribes multiplied and turned to an agricultural economy, this "rota" system broke down everywhere—with serious consequences. In twelfth-century Poland, for example, the branches of the ruling Piast family divided the country into virtually independent provinces (*Map 16*), leaving Silesia and Pomerania open to Germanization. In 1226, one of the Piast princelings invited the German Knights of the Cross (the Teutonic Order) to subdue the pagan Prussians. As a result, Poland lost her opportunity to colonize the Baltic littoral. In Kievan Rus, too, the central polity disintegrated as the rota system fell apart (*Map 14*). Members of the Rurik family established new and independent principalities west, north, and northeast of the Dnepr. Kiev's loss of authority was strikingly illustrated in 1169, when a prince of Rostov-Suzdal, Andrew Bogoliubski, sacked and pillaged the city, burning its monasteries and massacring its population. With power diffused among the many princes of Rus, Polovtsian tribes of the steppe were able to move across the Dnepr, cutting the water route from Kiev to Constantinople and splitting the Orthodox world in two (*Map 14*).

In Bohemia and Hungary, by way of contrast, the Přemyslid and Árpád dynasties maintained the outward integrity of their national territories in the centuries just before the Mongol attack (*Maps 16, 21*). But these lands were also weak politically. In Bohemia, the princes accepted a crown for the Czechs in 1086, not from the pope, but from the Holy Roman Emperor. This act symbolized the rapid pace at which princely disunity was leading Bohemia into the orbit of German politics. In Hungary, in the twelfth century, princely license was leading to another sort of peril. The Árpáds embarked on vast projects of purely dynastic expansion. To gain internal support, they made concessions to the barons of the kingdom, which culminated in 1222, when King Endre II issued a "Golden Bull" guaranteeing the nobles their "ancient" privileges and conceding them corporative powers to restrict the king's freedom of action.

The Tatar invasions resulted in drastic intensification of the trends already apparent in Russia and Hungary, the lands most directly affected, and in serious side effects in Poland and Bohemia.

In Rus, more than two centuries of the "Tatar Yoke" accentuated the divisions of the Russian people begun during the disintegration of Kievan Rus. In the south and west, where Tatar rule was relatively easy to escape, Russians accepted liberation during the fourteenth century through the alien and pagan agency of Lithuania (*Map 22*). Subsequently, they drifted with Lithuania under Polish-Catholic domination (*Map 26*). In the process, these Russians differentiated themselves sufficiently from the Great Russians of the north to deserve new generic names: They became the Ukrainians and Belorussians. Meanwhile, in the northeastern forest regions of Russia, where Tatar rule was exercised most forcibly, the many princes of Russia struggled for power (*Map 25*). Here the grand princes of Moscow fashioned a new power center and, after shrugging off the decaying Tatar authority late in the fifteenth century, made their goal the reassimilation of all the lost Russian lands. Moscow, the Russian center farthest removed geographically from Christian Europe, most intensively exposed to Mongol political models, and most fervently Orthodox in its faith, became the capital of a militant new Russian state.

In Hungary, the Tatar invasion decimated the Magyar peasantry and caused extensive population shifts (*Map 21*). The presence of Vlachs in Transylvania is recorded as early as 1209. In the century after the Tatar attack, the Vlachs moved down from the Carpathians into the depopulated valleys of Hungary and into the foothills south and east of the Carpathians, where they founded the principalities of Wallachia and Moldavia. More than ever before, the Kingdom of Hungary was a land of many nationalities.

A more subtle but equally important effect of the Tatar attack on Hungary was a further weakening of the position of the crown vis-à-vis its barons. When the last of the Árpáds died in 1301, the disposition of the throne fell to a nobility already as privileged as any in Europe; these nobles bestowed the crown upon the Neapolitan House of Anjou in exchange for confirmation of their rights. The Anjou kings of fourteenth-century Hungary took care to limit the powers of individual magnates, and they brought Hungary a century of stability. But they did not attempt to limit the rights of the nobility as a whole; instead, they devoted their talents even more than had the Árpáds to spectacular dynastic projects: the union of Hungary with Naples, with Poland (1370–82), and with Bohemia and the Holy Roman Empire (under Sigismund of Luxemburg in 1419–37) (*Maps 22, 23*).

These dynastic unions transmitted the Hungarian crown's weakness throughout Central Europe. Poland was most particularly affected. There the Tatar attack had been less devastating than in Hungary or Russia and had acted as a stimulus for revival of the national kingdom (*Map 18*). In 1370, Casimir the Great (1333–70), the last of the Piast kings, died. King Louis d'Anjou of Hungary inherited the throne and thereupon proclaimed, at Kassa (Košice) in 1374, a charter to the gentry of Poland that gave them all the rights of the Hungarian barony (*Maps 20, 22*). To the Poles, who recalled from recent experience the joys of provincial liberty, the Kassa Charter was heady wine. It inspired them in the following decades to take advantage of a national dilemma. At this time, German expansion was reaching its height in the Baltic (*Map 16*), and still-pagan Lithuania felt the Teutonic pressure most acutely. Therefore, in 1384, the Lithuanian grand prince, Jagiello, offered, in exchange for military aid, to accept Catholicism and to marry the daughter (then "king" of Poland) of King Louis, thus creating a personal union between Poland and Lithuania (*Map 22*). The Polish nobility accepted the offer, committing the country more than ever to a death struggle with the Teutonic Order that involved it in Russian affairs. But, in the wars that followed, the nobles repeatedly demanded further privileges from the king for their aid. The Jagiellon Dynasty, overwhelmed by the complexity of its enormous new Polish-Lithuanian realm, let the nobles have their way. By 1530, the weakness of Poland-Lithuania constituted a standing invitation to Russian expansionism (*Map 26*).

Bohemia was not ravished by the Mongols. Indeed, the thirteenth century brought it political stability, for the disintegration of the Holy Roman Empire gave renewed power to the Bohemian crown (*Map 23*). In the fourteenth century, under the Luxemburgian emperors, Bohemia became one of the principal political and cultural centers of Europe. After 1400, however, the religious, social, and national upheaval led by Jan Hus, the precursor of the European Reformation, disrupted this equilibrium, involving all social strata in Bohemia in internecine conflict. The last Luxemburgian emperor, Sigismund, was too engrossed in an ambitious effort to weld together a personal union of the Imperial, Hungarian, and Bohemian crowns to give adequate attention to the social problems of Bohemia. At his death in 1437, the Bohemian and Hungarian crowns fell jointly to members of the Habsburg family, already notorious in Central Europe for its tradition of accumulating new lands by an elaborate marriage policy. For twenty more years, under the Habsburgs, Bohemia had no firm governor. Meanwhile, the radical social elements supporting Hussitism were suppressed by the nobility, which swiftly increased its strength.

In 1458, both the Czechs and Hungarians elected native barons as kings, respectively George of Poděbrady (Jiři z Poděbrad) and Matthias Corvinus (Mátyás Hunyadi) (*Map 24*). At first, both seemed to promise the establishment of new, absolutist foundations for royal power. But neither succeeded, in part because Mátyás sought continuously to renew by force the union of Bohemia with Hungary. Upon the deaths of these rulers, first the Bohemian nobility, then the Hungarian, named as king not just a weak personality, but a Jagiellon who could be trusted to enlarge the local nobles' privileges to equal those of the Poles (*Map 26*). Thus, the weakening of the Hungarian crown by the Mongols in the thirteenth century contributed to the political disarray of all Northeastern Europe on the eve of 1500.

The Ottoman Turks reaped the profits of disarray in the Northeast, just as they had profited from the disaster of 1204 in the Southeast. The lands north of the Danube were fully conscious of the threat posed by the Islamic conquest of the Balkans, but they defended themselves only through two weak "crusades," one of which met defeat at Nikopolis in 1396, the other at Varna in 1443 (*Map 24*). The Mongol Tamerlane, who had no interest in Eastern Europe, did far more than these Europeans to break the Turkish advance (*Map 20*). He delayed the fall of Constantinople for fifty years by defeating the Turks at Ankara in 1402. After 1453, while the Turks were advancing northward to the Danube and the Black Sea steppe, Central Europe paid even less attention. The Hungarian nobility, for example, pursued its feudal interests to the extreme of eliminating a royal standing army altogether. The consequence was the defeat at Mohács in 1526, which gave most of Hungary to the Turks and its almost impotent crown, as well as Bohemia's, to a Habsburg Dynasty preoccupied with affairs in the West (*Map 33*).

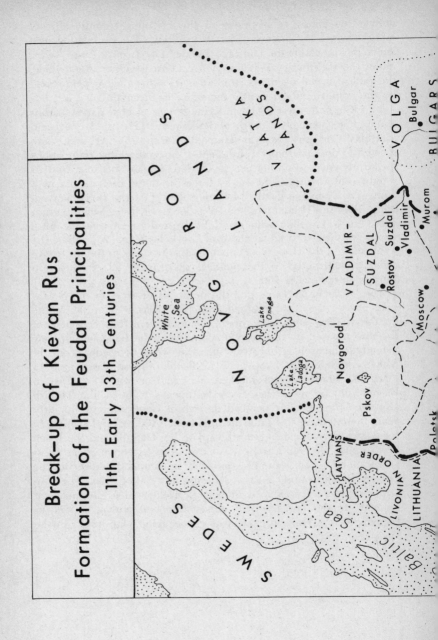

Break-up of Kievan Rus
Formation of the Feudal Principalities

11th – Early 13th Centuries

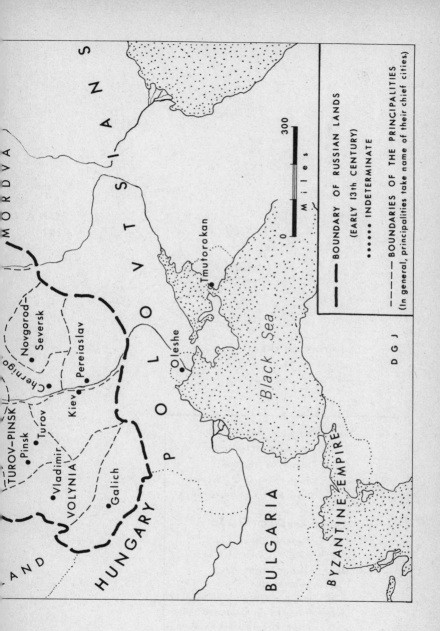

MORDVA

CARPATHIANS

TUROV-PINSK

Pinsk

Turov

Vladimir

VOLYNIA

Galich

Novgorod Seversk

Chernigo

Kiev Pereiaslav

POLAND

HUNGARY

POLOVTSI

Oleshe

Tmutorokan

Black Sea

BULGARIA

BYZANTINE EMPIRE

DGJ

BOUNDARY OF RUSSIAN LANDS
(EARLY 13th CENTURY)

••••• INDETERMINATE

BOUNDARIES OF THE PRINCIPALITIES
(In general, principalities take name of their chief cities)

0   300
Miles

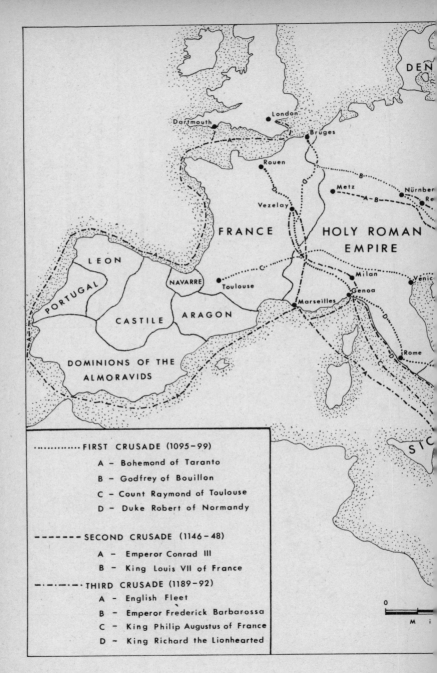

DEN

London
Dartmouth
Bruges

Rouen
Metz
Nürnber
A-B
Re
Vezelay

FRANCE
HOLY ROMAN
EMPIRE

LEON
C
Milan

NAVARRE
Venic

PORTUGAL
Toulouse
Genoa

Marseilles

CASTILE
ARAGON

Rome

DOMINIONS OF THE
ALMORAVIDS

SIC

.... FIRST CRUSADE (1095-99)

     A – Bohemond of Taranto

     B – Godfrey of Bouillon

     C – Count Raymond of Toulouse

     D – Duke Robert of Normandy

– – – – – SECOND CRUSADE (1146-48)

     A – Emperor Conrad III

     B – King Louis VII of France

–·–·–·– THIRD CRUSADE (1189-92)

     A – English Fleet

     B – Emperor Frederick Barbarossa

     C – King Philip Augustus of France

     D – King Richard the Lionhearted

0

M   i

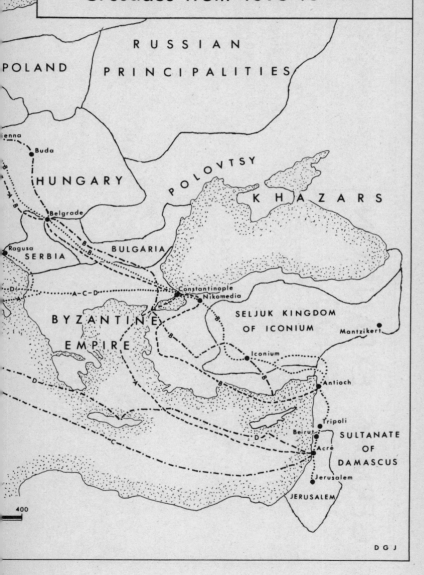

European Kingdoms About 1150
and the
Crusades from 1095 to 1192

POLAND

RUSSIAN

PRINCIPALITIES

Vienna

Buda

HUNGARY

POLOVTSY

KHAZARS

Belgrade

Ragusa

SERBIA

BULGARIA

Constantinople

Nikomedia

BYZANTINE

EMPIRE

SELJUK KINGDOM

OF ICONIUM

Mantzikert

Iconium

Antioch

Tripoli

Beirut

Acre

SULTANATE

OF

DAMASCUS

Jerusalem

JERUSALEM

400

D G J

GERMAN EXPANSION 850–1400

Narva

Reval

ESTONIA

BATTLE OF LAKE PEIPUS—1242

LIVONIA

Riga

COURLAND

SAMOGITIA

LITHUANIA

PRUSSIA

MASOVIA

Wisby

Danzig

POMERELIA

POMERANIA
(12th–13th Cent.)

MECKLENBURG

BRANDENBURG
(12th Cent.)

GREAT POLAND

LUSATIA

Breslau

Lübeck

DENMARK

Hamburg

Magdeburg

THURINGIA

Meissen

SAXONY

Köln

200

0

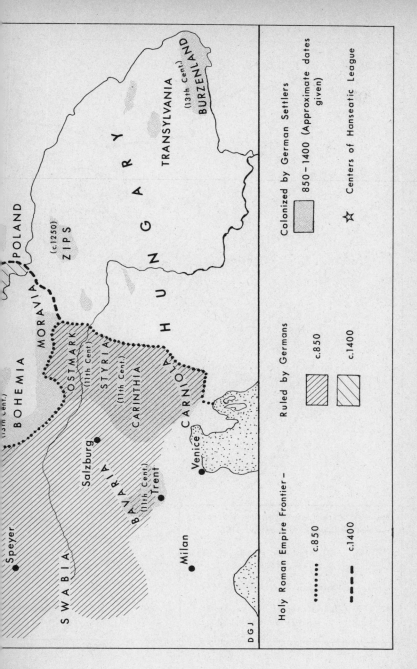

POLAND

BOHEMIA
(13th Cent.)

MORAVIA

ZIPS
(c.1250)

OSTMARK
(11th Cent.)

STYRIA
(11th Cent.)

CARINTHIA

CARNIO

HUNGARY

TRANSYLVANIA

BURZENLAND
(13th Cent.)

Speyer

SWABIA

BAVARIA

Salzburg

Trent
(11th Cent.)

Milan

Venice

D G J

Holy Roman Empire Frontier—

c.850

c.1400

Ruled by Germans

c.850

c.1400

Colonized by German Settlers

850–1400 (Approximate dates given)

☆ Centers of Hanseatic League

47

HUNGARIAN LANDS

RAMA

Ras

Ragusa

SERBIA

Trnovo

BULGARIA

Klokotnica
(1230)

Dyrrachion

Adrianople

Bari

Ochrida

EMPIRE

DESPOT

Thessalonika

OF

OF

CONSTANT

EPIRUS

KINGDOM OF THESSALONIKA

DUCHY
OF
ATHENS

EMP

PRINCIPALITY
OF
ACHAEA

Candia

Greatest Extent of Byzantine Suzerainty
—— Under Manuel I – 1180

Still in Greek Hands
c. 1214

.... Venetian Possesions – c.1214

Despotate of Epirus at Its
Greatest Extent – 1220
☆ Battle

0
M

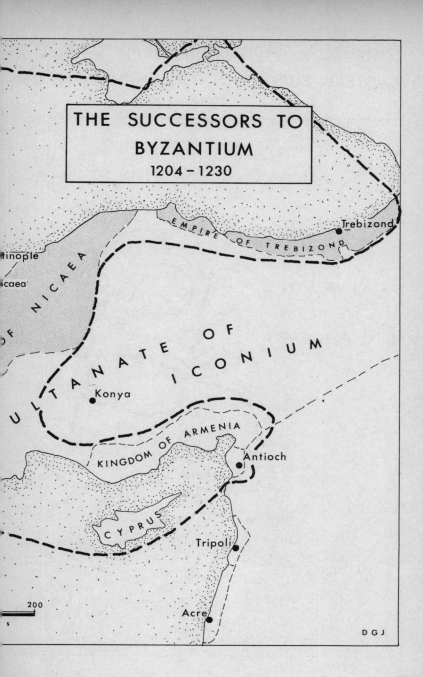

THE SUCCESSORS TO
BYZANTIUM
1204 – 1230

tinople

caea

EMPIRE OF TREBIZOND

Trebizond

OF NICAEA

ULTANATE OF ICONIUM

Konya

KINGDOM OF ARMENIA

Antioch

CYPRUS

Tripoli

200

S

Acre

DGJ

49

THE MONGOL INVASION OF RUSSIA AN
EASTERN EUROPE IN THE THIRTEENTH CENT
1241 – 1263

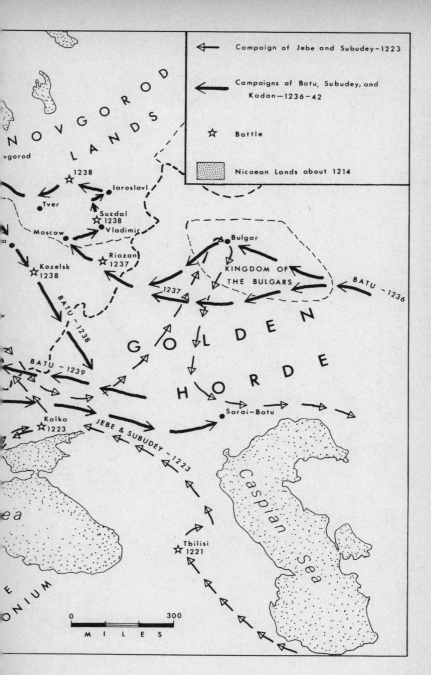

Campaign of Jebe and Subudey—1223

Campaigns of Batu, Subudey, and Kadan—1236–42

☆ Battle

Nicaean Lands about 1214

NOVGOROD LANDS

vgorod

1238

Tver

Iaroslavl

Moscow
Suzdal
1238
Vladimir

Kozelsk
1238

Riazan
1237

BATU – 1238

Bulgar

KINGDOM OF
THE BULGARS

1237

BATU – 1236

G O L D E N

H O R D E

BATU – 1239

Kalka
1223

JEBE & SUBUDEY – 1223

Sarai-Batu

Caspian Sea

ea

Tbilisi
1221

0   300

M I L E S

ONIUM

51

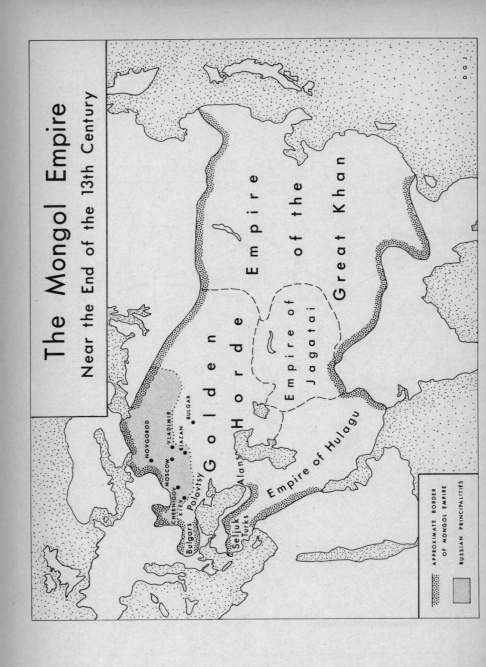

The Mongol Empire
Near the End of the 13th Century

Empire of the Great Khan

Golden Horde Empire

Empire of Jagatai

Empire of Hulagu

NOVGOROD

VLADIMIR
MOSCOW
CHERNIGOV
RIAZAN
KIEV
BULGAR
Bulgars
Polovtsy
Alans
Seljuk
Turks

APPROXIMATE BORDER
OF MONGOL EMPIRE

RUSSIAN PRINCIPALITIES

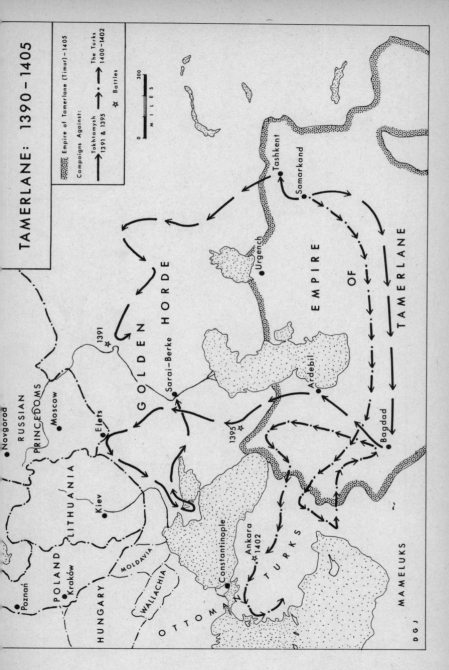

TAMERLANE: 1390–1405

Empire of Tamerlane (Timur) – 1405

Campaigns Against:

Tokhtamysh
1391 & 1395

The Turks
1400–1402

☆ Battles

0   300

M I L E S

Novgorod

RUSSIAN
PRINCEDOMS

Moscow

1391 ☆

Elets

POLAND

Poznań

Kraków

LITHUANIA

Kiev

HUNGARY

MOLDAVIA

WALLACHIA

Constantinople

Ankara
1402 ☆

OTTOMAN
TURKS

Sarai-Berke

GOLDEN   HORDE

1395 ☆

Urgench

Tashkent

Samarkand

EMPIRE

OF

TAMERLANE

Ardebil

Bagdad

MAMELUKS

D G J

MAP 20   /53

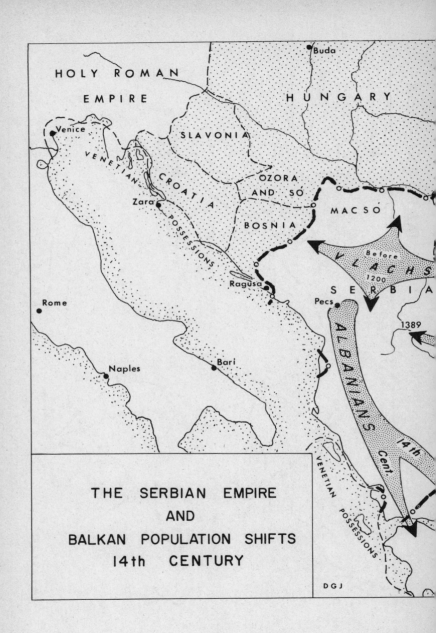

THE SERBIAN EMPIRE
AND
BALKAN POPULATION SHIFTS
14th CENTURY

DGJ

1349

MOLDAVIA   GOLDEN HORDE

09

VLACHS

1290

WALLACHIA

SERBIA AND HER
BULGARIAN VASSAL (1355)

HUNGARY AND HER VASSALS
(14th CENTURY)

BULGARIA

Philippopolis

1363

Maritza R.

BYZANTIUM

Constantinopole

Nikomedia
1337

nike

Athos

Gallipolis
1354

TURKS

SELJUK   TURKS

ETIAN

POSSESSIONS

0   100   200

MILES

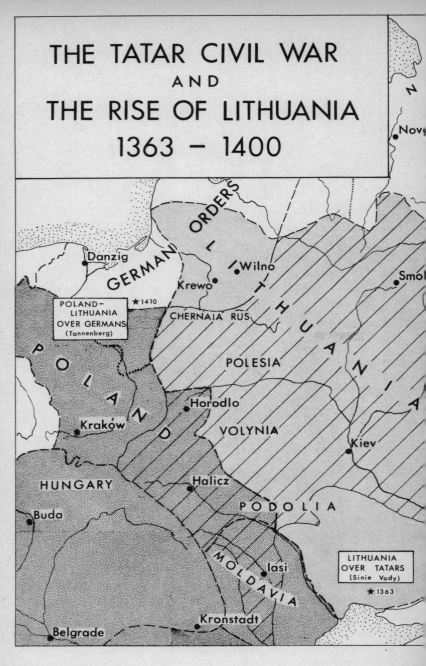

THE TATAR CIVIL WAR
AND
THE RISE OF LITHUANIA
1363 – 1400

Nov

Danzig

GERMAN ORDERS

L

Wilno

Krewo

Smo

POLAND–
LITHUANIA
OVER GERMANS
(Tannenberg)

★ 1410

CHERNAIA RUS

POLAND

POLESIA

L
I
T
H
U
A
N
I
A

Kraków

Horodlo

VOLYNIA

Kiev

HUNGARY

Halicz

PODOLIA

Buda

MOLDAVIA

Iasi

LITHUANIA
OVER TATARS
(Sinie Vody)

★ 1363

Kronstadt

Belgrade

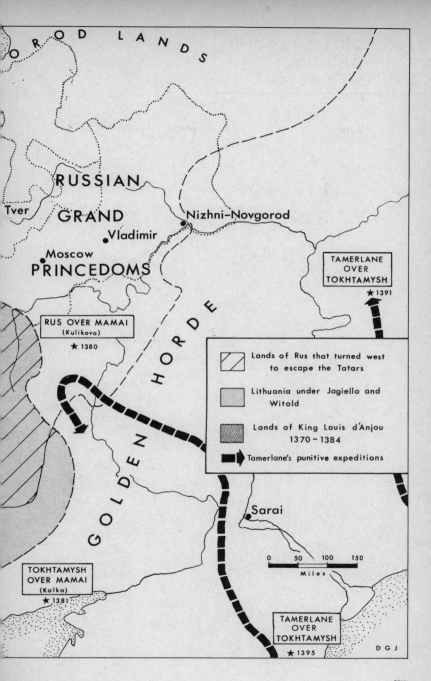

RUSSIAN GRAND PRINCEDOMS

NOVGOROD LANDS

Tver

Moscow

Vladimir

Nizhni-Novgorod

GOLDEN HORDE

Sarai

RUS OVER MAMAI
(Kulikovo)
★ 1380

TOKHTAMYSH OVER MAMAI
(Kalka)
★ 1381

TAMERLANE OVER TOKHTAMYSH
★ 1391

TAMERLANE OVER TOKHTAMYSH
★ 1395

Lands of Rus that turned west to escape the Tatars

Lithuania under Jagiello and Witold

Lands of King Louis d'Anjou 1370–1384

Tamerlane's punitive expeditions

0   50   100   150
Miles

D G J

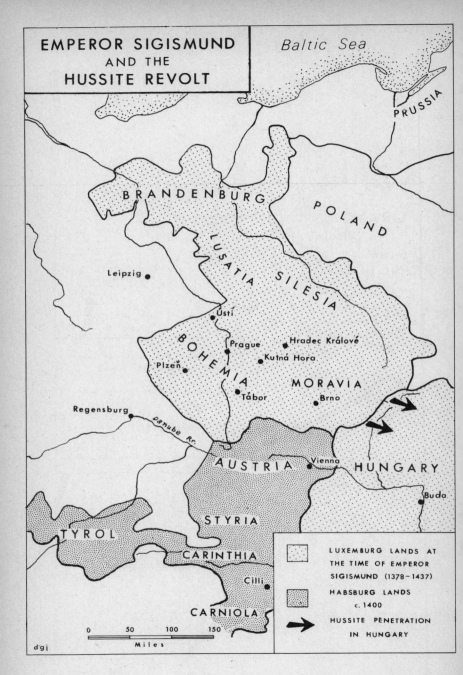

EMPEROR SIGISMUND
AND THE
HUSSITE REVOLT

Baltic Sea

PRUSSIA

B R A N D E N B U R G

P O L A N D

LUSATIA

SILESIA

Leipzig

Ústí

BOHEMIA

Prague

Hradec Králové

Kutná Hora

Plzeň

MORAVIA

Tábor

Brno

Regensburg

Danube R.

AUSTRIA

Vienna

HUNGARY

STYRIA

Buda

TYROL

CARINTHIA

Cilli

CARNIOLA

LUXEMBURG LANDS AT
THE TIME OF EMPEROR
SIGISMUND (1378-1437)

HABSBURG LANDS
c. 1400

HUSSITE PENETRATION
IN HUNGARY

0   50   100   150
Miles

d'gi

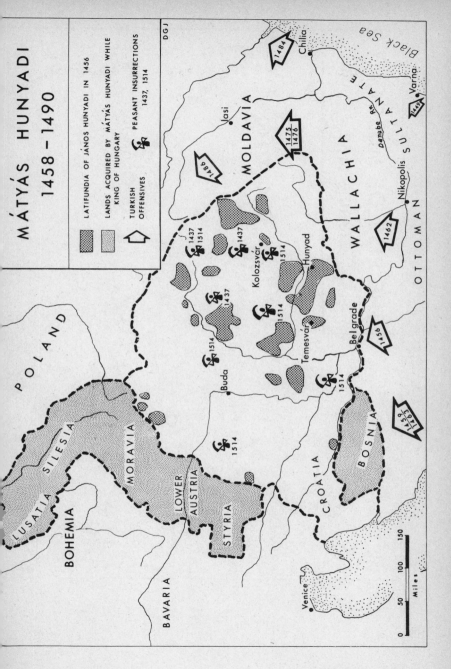

MÁTYÁS HUNYADI
1458–1490

LATIFUNDIA OF JÁNOS HUNYADI IN 1456

LANDS ACQUIRED BY MÁTYÁS HUNYADI WHILE KING OF HUNGARY

PEASANT INSURRECTIONS
1437, 1514

TURKISH OFFENSIVES

DGJ

POLAND

BOHEMIA

LUSATIA

SILESIA

MORAVIA

LOWER AUSTRIA

STYRIA

BAVARIA

MOLDAVIA

Iasi

WALLACHIA

Danube R.

Chilia

Varna

Black Sea

Nikopolis

OTTOMAN SULTANATE

1484

1486

1475 1476

1462

1468

1456

1463 1459

1437 1514

1437

1514

1437

1514

1514

1514

1514

Kolozsvár

Hunyad

Temesvár

Belgrade

Buda

CROATIA

BOSNIA

Venice

Miles

0   50   100   150

MAP 24 / **59**

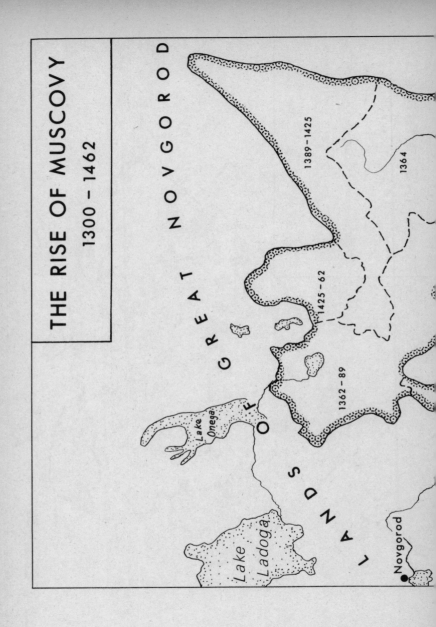

THE RISE OF MUSCOVY
1300 – 1462

GREAT NOVGOROD

1389–1425

1364

1425–62

1362–89

Lake Onega

OF

Lake Ladoga

LANDS

● Novgorod

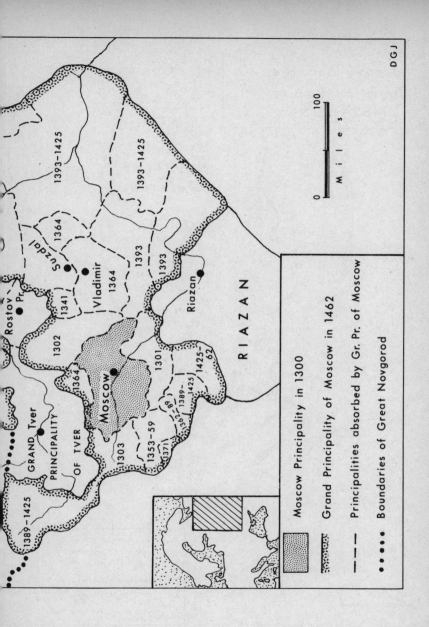

GRAND PRINCIPALITY OF TVER

PRINCIPALITY OF TVER

1389–1425

Rostov Pr.

Suzdal

1393–1425

1393–1425

1364

1341

1364

1302

Vladimir
1364

1393

1393

Moscow

1364

1303

1353–59

1371

1362–89

1389–

1425

1301

1425–
62

Riazan

RIAZAN

Miles

0   100

Moscow Principality in 1300

Grand Principality of Moscow in 1462

Principalities absorbed by Gr. Pr. of Moscow

Boundaries of Great Novgorod

DGJ

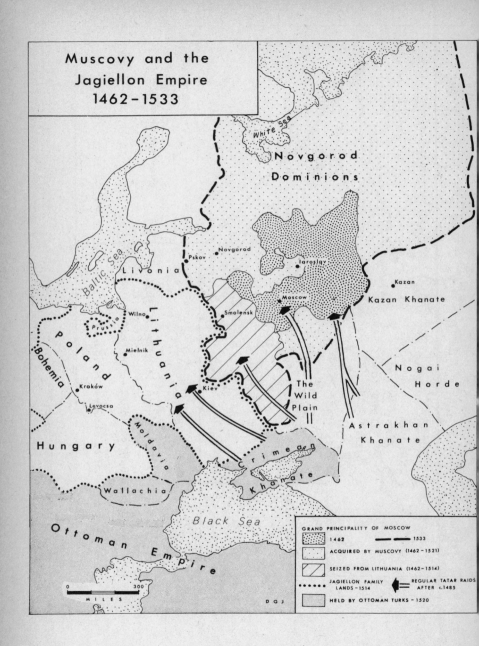

Muscovy and the Jagiellon Empire 1462–1533

White Sea

Novgorod Dominions

Baltic Sea

Livonia

Pskov · Novgorod

Iaroslav ·

Kazan ·

Moscow ·

Kazan Khanate

Prussia

Wilno ·

Smolensk ·

Poland

Lithuania

Mielnik ·

Bohemia

Kraków ·

Kiev ·

The Wild Plain

Nogai Horde

Astrakhan Khanate

Levocsa ·

Hungary

Moldavia

Crimean Khanate

Wallachia

Black Sea

Ottoman Empire

GRAND PRINCIPALITY OF MOSCOW

1462 — 1533

ACQUIRED BY MUSCOVY (1462–1521)

SEIZED FROM LITHUANIA (1462–1514)

JAGIELLON FAMILY LANDS –1514

REGULAR TATAR RAIDS AFTER c.1485

HELD BY OTTOMAN TURKS –1520

0 ——— 300

MILES

D G J

The Economic and Social Blight of Early Modern Eastern Europe and Russia (MAPS 27–30)

A blight afflicted the economies and societies of the eastern parts of Europe at the dawn of the modern era.

One reason for this blight was the inherent agricultural weakness of Eastern Europe as compared to the West. The mountainous Balkans and the dry, cold, forested areas of Eastern Europe and Russia were more difficult to cultivate and, for the most part, much less fruitful than the well-watered lowlands of the Atlantic countries and Italy. Before the fourteenth century, the potential consequences of these natural shortcomings were blurred. With even the crudest of implements, the agricultural populations of the eastern lands were able to survive by constantly shifting from exhausted fields to virgin lands; also, new techniques introduced from the West (the moldboard plow and the draining of marshlands) brought momentary increases of productivity and helped to hide the fundamental disabilities of agriculture in the eastern lands. German immigration was important in this respect (*Map 16*). By the fourteenth century, however, a number of economic and social developments in Eastern and Western Europe sharply worsened a situation already made difficult by poor soil, bad climate, and primitive agricultural techniques.

A second reason for the blight lay in the coincidence of the growing economic dynamism of the West with political disasters that destroyed the trading centers of the East. The twelfth century, which saw the revival of commerce in the West, brought, in the East, the capture of Byzantium's trade by Italian merchants and the sack of Constantinople by the Latin crusaders (*Maps 15, 17*). In the thirteenth century, Baltic trade was captured by the German and Flemish Hanseatic League at the very time that such cities as Kiev and Buda were ravished by the Tatar invasions (*Maps 16, 18*). In the fourteenth and fifteenth centuries, some Eastern European towns—for example, Novgorod, Danzig, Kraków, and Prague—still ranked among the most prosperous centers of Europe; and the mining districts of Hungary, Bohemia, and Poland were great sources of wealth (*Map 29*). But after 1400, while the West was recovering from its late medieval economic depression, the Hussite wars weakened Prague (*Map 23*); the Muscovite Grand Prince Ivan III seized Novgorod and closed down its trade with the Germans (*Map 26*); and Turkish expansion threatened Hungary and cut the trade routes across the Black Sea that had fed Kraków

(*Maps 24, 26*). Thus, even before 1500, when the new sea routes to India caused the decisive shift of European trade from the Mediterranean and Germany to the Atlantic, Eastern Europe and Russia had become trading backwaters (*Map 30*).

The third important cause of the social and economic blight of early modern Eastern Europe and Russia was the universal introduction of serfdom in those lands during the fourteenth, fifteenth, and sixteenth centuries (*Map 28*). Serfdom was the systematic binding of the farming population to the soil it cultivated so that it might be more effectively exploited by the master of the land than could a population free to depart at will. In return for his services, the serf usually received a small share of the fruits of his labor; the major share went to his master. Serfdom differed from slavery in that the peasant or serf was bound to the land by a variety of obligations or by law. Unlike the slave, he was usually considered a member of society, and this gave him some rights to the land he tilled as well as the duty to pay taxes.

Serfdom was endemic in agricultural areas throughout ancient times, and it became almost universal in the early medieval West. This occurred not because it was recognized as an objectively profitable system, but because the Roman state authority had disappeared in the West; the agricultural population was able to survive the anarchy of the times only by binding itself to warrior landlords who obliged themselves to defend it. This situation lasted in the West only until the eleventh and twelfth centuries, when public order returned and serfdom could be replaced by more productive agricultural systems. Thereafter, in the later medieval centuries, serf obligations gave way increasingly to contractual relationships between lords and free peasants that involved payments of fees or rents with money or services.

Among the reasons for the introduction of serfdom in the eastern parts of Europe, one of the first was imitation of the feudalism practiced in the West and Byzantium. One after another, the Central and Eastern European societies systematically replaced their old tribal relationships and administrative systems with the feudal institutions of the French. After the union of Poland and Lithuania, at the turn of the fifteenth century, feudal institutions were introduced in the western Russian lands under Lithuanian rule. Everywhere one result of the importation of feudalism was the arbitrary division of once-free tribal societies into servile (serf) and noble (military) classes.

Another factor in the development of serfdom was the general shortage of agricultural labor. This was, perhaps, the most important influence in Russia, where labor shortages at first tended to prolong the existence of a free peasantry that farmed princely or boyar estates. However, this freedom was in some sense illusory, since many of these "free" farmers were actually bound to the land by debts. In the sixteenth century, when Russia's peasants had learned to flee their debts and seek real freedom in the frontier areas on the steppe, the Tsars took legal measures to assure their return and to bind them to the land.

Other elements facilitated the universal growth of Eastern European serfdom. In Eastern Europe, for example, towns did not play the great role in the development of society that they played in the West; they were in no position to resist the development of serfdom. Similarly, kings in the East were nowhere as independent of the nobility as were kings in the West; they were unable to protect the peasant. In Russia, the development of the Muscovite state involved the grand princes in vicious and costly struggles against the arrogant claims of subject nobles, whose willfulness crippled Muscovite authority. To win these struggles, the grand princes abandoned the peasantry to the nobles' systematic exploitation.

The universal establishment of serfdom was climaxed in the fifteenth, sixteenth, and seventeenth centuries by three significant developments (*Map 28*). First, as the Ottoman Turks conquered the Balkans they abolished all the old social forms and imposed their own absolutist brand of serfdom (*Maps 21, 24*). Second, the Muscovite grand princes sought to replace their troublesome hereditary nobility with a new and subservient service class—the *dvorianstvo* or *pomeshchiki*—men who were wholly dependent upon the small estates granted by the grand prince and who, therefore, demanded that the peasants be forced by law to remain on the land (*Maps 25, 37*). Third, the rise of large urban centers in Western Europe led to a demand for grain. Western traders, particularly the Dutch, established direct contact with the richer landowners of Northeastern Europe, encouraging them to found huge grain-producing farms—latifundia (*Map 30; see also 24*). As it happened, this sort of production was well suited to the cool, dry plains of the East, and it could be operated profitably with serf labor. Thus, the development of latifundia further extended serfdom.

Many islands of relative prosperity remained in Eastern Europe in the sixteenth century. But the general picture was one of decaying trade and rigidifying serfdom, which, together with the fundamental agricultural weaknesses of the area and the social conditions of the time, contributed to the spread of poverty and fear among nobles and peasants alike.

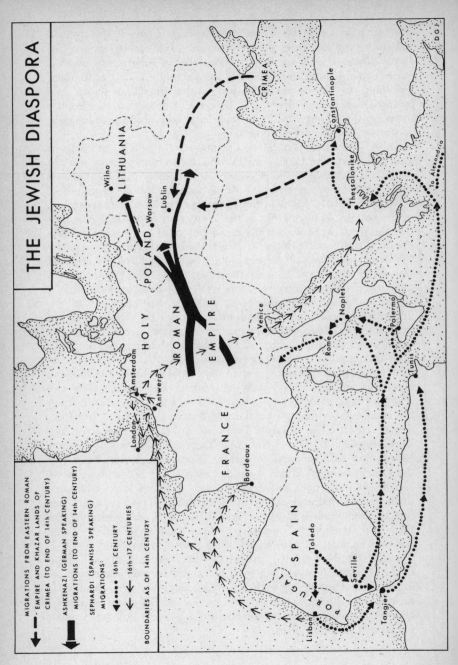

THE JEWISH DIASPORA

CRIMEA

LITHUANIA
Wilno

Lublin
Warsaw
POLAND

HOLY
ROMAN

EMPIRE

Amsterdam
Antwerp
London

FRANCE

Bordeaux

SPAIN

PORTUGAL

Toledo
Seville
Lisbon
Tangier

Venice
Rome
Naples
Palermo

Tunis

Constantinople
Thessalonike
To Alexandria

D.G.J.

MIGRATIONS FROM EASTERN ROMAN
EMPIRE AND KHAZAR LANDS OF
CRIMEA (TO END OF 14th CENTURY)

ASHKENAZI (GERMAN SPEAKING)
MIGRATIONS (TO END OF 14th CENTURY)

SEPHARDI (SPANISH SPEAKING)
MIGRATIONS:

●●●●● 16th CENTURY

16th–17 CENTURIES

BOUNDARIES AS OF 14th CENTURY

EXTENSION OF SERFDOM IN EASTERN EUROPE

LIVONIA 1562

16th Century Wars

MOSCOW
1497, 1550, 1597

Rise of Military State

Scarcity of Labor

Decline of Teutonic Order

Decline of Hanse Towns

LITHUANIA
1505, 1569

PRUSSIA 1526

Grain Trade with Dutch Encourages Latifundia Agriculture

Polish Example

POLAND
1496,   1518

Peasant War 1525

UKRAINE
17th & 18th Centuries

BOHEMIA
1472, 1500

Constitutional Rise of Gentry, Decline of the Crown, and the Decline of Towns

Polish – Russian Colonization

Decline of Cossacks

Hussite War

HUNGARY
1351, 1437, 1515

MOLDAVIA
1621

Punishment of Peasant Rebels

WALLACHIA 1595

Military Needs

Ottoman Invasions 14th–16th Centuries

- Frontiers as of about 1500.

- Dates refer to important serf legislation.

- Insets suggest milestones on the road to serfdom.

DGJ

MAP 28   / 67

Bremen — Main Hanseatic Centers

London — Foreign Offices of Hansa

•••••• — Trade Area of Hansa

• — Main Trade Centers

←——← — Direction of Major Trade Routes

Bergen

COPP

TIMBER

TAR

Oslo

Sto

FLAX

IRON

Copenhagen

Hamburg

Lübeck

FIS

Bremen

D

Brunswick

Magdebu

London

WOOL

TIN

Bruges

Cologne

WOOLENS

Paris

WINE

WOOLENS

Prague

LINEN

Nürnberg

SILVER

CHAMPAGNE

Augsburg

GRAIN

Loire Rr.

Rhine Rr.

Lyons

Bordeaux

WINE

Rhone Rr.

Venice

Genoa

IRON

Leon

Marseilles

Rome

WOOL

Barcelona

Naples

Lisbon

Toledo

LEAD

Córdoba

OLIVE OIL

Palermo

SILK

SILK

GRAIN

WOOL

Tunis

DATES

SALT

GOLD

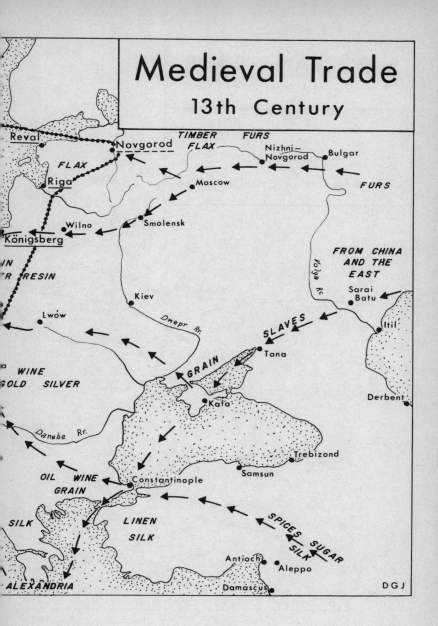

Medieval Trade
13th Century

Reval
Novgorod
TIMBER   FURS
FLAX
FLAX
Riga
Moscow
Nizhni–
Novgorod
Bulgar
FURS
Wilno
Smolensk
Königsberg
IN
R RESIN
Kiev
Lwów
Dnepr Rr.
Volga Rr.
FROM CHINA
AND THE
EAST
Sarai
Batu
Itil
SLAVES
Tana
GRAIN
Kafa
Derbent
WINE
GOLD   SILVER
Danube   Rr.
Trebizond
OIL   WINE
Samsun
GRAIN
Constantinople
SILK
LINEN
SILK
SPICES SUGAR
SILK
Antioch
Aleppo
ALEXANDRIA
Damascus

DGJ

69

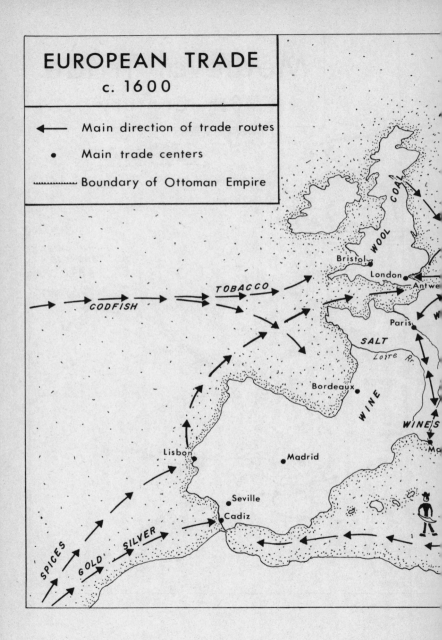

EUROPEAN TRADE
c. 1600

← Main direction of trade routes

• Main trade centers

········· Boundary of Ottoman Empire

WOOL

COAL

Bristol

London

Antwe

TOBACCO

CODFISH

Paris

SALT

Loire R.

Bordeaux

WINE

WINES

Lisbon

Madrid

Ma

Seville

Cadiz

SPICES

GOLD

SILVER

Part III

Eastern Europe and Russia During the European Renaissance

By 1500, Western Europe was emerging from the isolation of its medieval period and embarking on that discovery of the rest of the world and of classical learning that historians term the Renaissance. By 1815, a dynamic Western Europe had achieved, through intellectual and technological revolutions, new cultural, economic, and political forms and conquests of many parts of the world. Eastern Europe and, to a limited extent, Russia shared in the first flowering of the Renaissance, and several of the eastern lands made distinctive contributions to it; but long before 1815, it was evident that the eastern regions were not sharing fully in the West's continuing progress. In 1815, the three great eastern powers—Austria, Prussia, and Russia—played major political roles in Western Europe and, with the other eastern lands, they formed a part of the European community. Nevertheless, a cultural gap divided West from East. The West was "advanced," the East "backward."

Cultural Stagnation and Wars (MAPS 31–40)

One major reason why the East did not develop along with the West after 1500 were the political disasters, comparable to those of the thirteenth century, that seared Eastern Europe in the sixteenth and seventeenth centuries. On the one hand, state-imposed cultural orthodoxy suffocated centers of Renaissance thought, particularly in Russia and in the lands newly won by the Ottoman Turks. On the other hand, prolonged and devastating wars wrecked almost all the lands of the East, retarding their economic development and greatly intensifying social and political ills.

In point of time, one of the first of the East's setbacks, stemming from a change in the character of the Ottoman Empire, affected the Balkans. Until the conquest of the Near East by Selim I (1512–20), Ottoman power, centered in the Balkan Peninsula, was relatively open to Western ideas (*Map 34*). The sultans accepted a flexible interpretation of Islam; they virtually excluded the Moslem religious community from government by ruling through a slave bureaucracy and a slave army recruited largely in Christian lands; and they permitted the Christian communities within their territories considerable autonomy. But in the reign of Suleiman the Lawgiver (or the Magnificent, 1520–66), the Ottomans turned to the rigid and legalistic orthodoxy of the Sunna religious sect. This trend was spurred by the emergence in Persia after 1500 of a rival Islamic political center dominated by the messianic Shiah religious group. Meanwhile, the enormous size of the Ottoman Empire and the economic difficulties created by the shift of East-West trade routes away from the Mediterranean (*Map 30*) led to a deterioration of the slave system of administration. Profiting from these troubles and from a succession of weak sultans, the Moslem religious community penetrated the government and the army, establishing, in effect, a theocracy. In the seventeenth and eighteenth centuries, the Empire dedicated itself to sterile and corrupt changelessness, rejecting all opportunities to grow with the West or to learn from it.

Moscow also turned to religious obscurantism during the early Renaissance. It did so, at first, in order to resist nationalistic and Protestant religious movements such as that introduced by the "Judaizers," who appeared in Novgorod about 1470 and whose ideas became influential in Muscovy after Ivan III conquered Novgorod (*Map 26*). The Muscovite Church set itself to preserve its own interpretation of Russian Orthodoxy as the one true religion, making even the suggestion of innovation in the faith, the state order, or learning an act of heresy. The Tsars accepted this interpretation, partly because of their fear of being condemned as heretics and partly because they needed the Church's support. By the late sixteenth century, the Russian theocracy had frozen intellectual and cultural affairs into officially approved molds.

Meanwhile, great wars began to smother the active Renaissance centers of Eastern Europe. In fifteenth-century Hungary, the court at Buda shared with much of Europe an interest in the new culture of Italy (*Map 31*). But in 1541, the Turks sacked Buda and drove the court, greatly impoverished, to Vienna and Transylvania (*Maps 33, 35*). Yet, despite this setback, Hungary remained a European cultural center throughout the sixteenth century, and as the Reformation advanced, Transylvania became one of the principal islands of religious and intellectual tolerance on the continent (*Map 32*). But between 1591 and 1606, disaster struck again. One after another, Imperial, Ottoman, Vlach, and native armies coursed through the fertile valleys, living off the land (*Map 35*). Politically, Transylvania still maintained its sovereignty in the first part of the seventeenth century, but the defeat of its armies in Poland in 1657 brought about its collapse (*Maps 39, 40*). Nor was Hungary's trial over even then. For almost thirty years after 1683, Habsburg armies lived off the land while "liberating" Hungary from the Turks (*Map 46*).

Like Hungary, the frontier lands of the Ottoman Empire, Poland-Lithuania, and Muscovy all endured military devastation after 1500. With the approach of the Turks late in the fifteenth century, the Crimean Tatars ceased helping Genoese merchants to collect grain from the steppe for Mediterranean cities and began collecting slaves for Istanbul (*Maps 26, 30*). In the century between 1474 and their sack of Moscow in 1571, the Crimean Tatars invaded Lithuanian and Muscovite borderlands again and again, dragging away thousands of captives for the slave markets. In this same era, an ever greater number of peasants fled to the southern steppe, hoping to escape the oppressions of serfdom in Poland-Lithuania and Muscovy (*Map 28*). Pursuing them, Polish nobles and Muscovite armies extended serfdom and established tenuous controls over the free steppe cultures along the lower Dnepr and Volga rivers (*Maps 36, 37*).

At the turn of the seventeenth century, Russia suffered its "Time of Troubles" (1598–1613) (*Map 38*). The conduct of Ivan the Terrible's retainers, as well as his own mad efforts to reconstruct the whole of Russian society in a way that would give him absolute power, had depopulated vast areas of central Russia, exacerbating already difficult social conflicts. With the death of Ivan's son Feodor (1598), the dynasty of Rurik came to an end. Torn by dissentient claimants to the throne, the nation began to fall apart, and Polish and Swedish armies seized this opportunity to invade. Hordes of uprooted, hungry peasants and Cossacks, led by Polish and Russian pretenders to the throne, nobles, and simple bandits, straggled across the land, sacking towns and estates, burning villages, and slaughtering one another. The destruction that resulted before Michael Romanov was elected to the Muscovite throne in 1613 left Russia exhausted and impoverished.

By weakening the obscurantist Orthodox theocracy and by demonstrating the inability of Muscovite ideas and institutions to provide effective means of preserving the nation, the Time of Troubles may have saved Russia from the kind of stagnation that was to destroy the Ottoman Empire. Perhaps the very intensity of the crisis and the long search for a way out of it made possible the willingness to look westward for ideas that later, under Peter the Great (1689–1725), grew into an overwhelming determination.

Bohemia and Poland seemed, until the seventeenth century, to be integral parts of the Western cultural development. Indeed, Prague, one of the centers of late medieval European art, was the locus of the first European religious reformation (led by John Hus) and, in 1600, the effective capital of the German Empire (*Maps 31, 32; see also 23*). Poland, in the sixteenth century, was a center of Italianate culture and ranked with Transylvania as a center of religious tolerance (*Maps 31, 32*). But early in the seventeenth century, political disasters overtook these lands.

Bohemia was the first to fall. Step by step, during the sixteenth century, its position had weakened as its society and Habsburg rulers became pillars of the Counter Reformation (*Map 33*). In 1618, the Protestant Estates of Bohemia expelled the Catholic Habsburgs, thus launching the Thirty Years' War (*Map 39*). Two years later, Bohemia lost its independence at the Battle of the White Mountain, outside Prague. In the decades that followed, all of neighboring Germany was ravaged by massive armies and, consequently, was set back culturally and economically. Bohemia was the only major Protestant part of Central Europe to fall completely into Catholic Imperial hands. When the Protestant Czech nobility had to flee from political oppression and religious persecution, the nation was deprived of an educated leadership, and its native culture faded. Thus, Bohemia suffered from the military effects of the struggle as well as its spiritual consequences.

Poland, last of the Eastern European nations to experience the turmoil of the Renaissance period, at first suffered an internal decay. As early as 1574, shortly after Poland's final absorption of Lithuania at Lublin, an elected king, Henri de Valois, humiliated the nation by running away to accept the crown of France. Thereafter, the Polish nobility irresponsibly demolished the crown's remaining powers. Long before 1648, the Polish-Lithuanian Union had become powerless to act without the nobles' assembly (*Sejm*). The Sejm itself was soon paralyzed by the *liberum veto*—the right of any member to block any measure under consideration and to void the entire accomplishment of the assembly by saying, "I forbid." Meanwhile, in the one area where the crown could still move with relative freedom—religion—it loosed a counterreformation that attacked not only Protestants but also the Orthodox Russian population of Lithuania.

In 1648, the treaties of Westphalia ended the German wars and freed Poland's northern neighbor, Sweden, for new expansion (*Map 39*). In the same year, the "Polish Deluge" began with an uprising of Orthodox Cossacks and peasants of the Polish steppe (*Map 40*). Led by Bogdan Khmelnitsky and joined by the Tatars, these forces burned and massacred their way through southern Lithuania and Poland. The Deluge continued with repeated invasions by Russia, Sweden, Brandenburg, Transylvania, and the Turks. Beset from all sides, Poland was a battlefield from 1648 until the end of the struggle between Peter the Great and Sweden in 1721 (*Map 43*).

At the beginning of the eighteenth century, after the Deluge, Poland remained only relatively healthier than the devastated lands of the Balkans, the Ukraine, and Hungary. No more than the other lands of the East was it in a position to share in the cultural dynamism of the West.

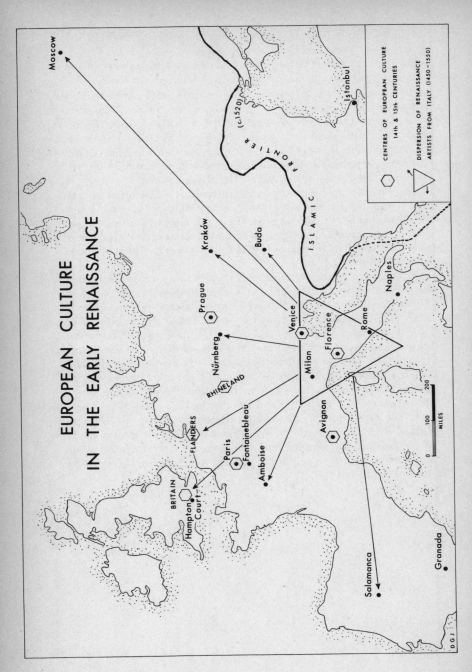

EUROPEAN CULTURE
IN THE EARLY RENAISSANCE

CENTERS OF EUROPEAN CULTURE
14th & 15th CENTURIES

DISPERSION OF RENAISSANCE
ARTISTS FROM ITALY (1450-1550)

Moscow

Istanbul

FRONTIER (c.1520)

ISLAMIC

Kraków

Buda

Naples

Prague

Nürnberg

Venice

Florence

Rome

Milan

RHINELAND

Avignon

FLANDERS

Paris

Fontainebleau

Amboise

BRITAIN

Hampton Court

Salamanca

Granada

0   100   200
MILES

D.G.J.

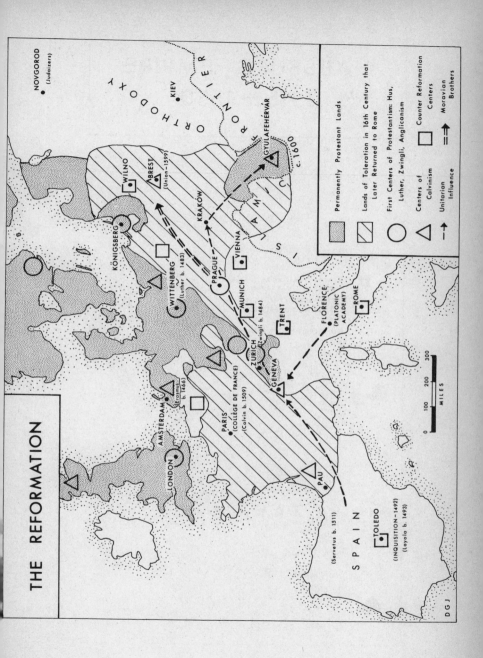

THE REFORMATION

Legend:
- Permanently Protestant Lands
- Lands of Toleration in 16th Century that Later Returned to Rome
- First Centers of Protestantism: Hus, Luther, Zwingli, Anglicanism
- Centers of Calvinism
- Counter Reformation Centers
- Unitarian Influence
- Moravian Brothers

NOVGOROD (Judaizers)

KIEV

ORTHODOXY

FRONTIER

WILNO

BREST (Union-1599)

KRAKÓW

GYULAFEHÉRVÁR

I S L A M c. 1600

KÖNIGSBERG

WITTENBERG (Luther b. 1483)

PRAGUE

VIENNA

MUNICH

ZÜRICH (Zwingli b. 1484)

TRENT

FLORENCE (PLATONIC ACADEMY)

ROME

GENEVA

AMSTERDAM (Erasmus b. 1466)

PARIS (COLLÈGE DE FRANCE) (Calvin b. 1509)

LONDON

PAU

(Servetus b. 1511)

S P A I N

TOLEDO (INQUISITION-1492) (Loyola b. 1493)

0   100   200   300
MILES

DGJ

MAP 32   /79

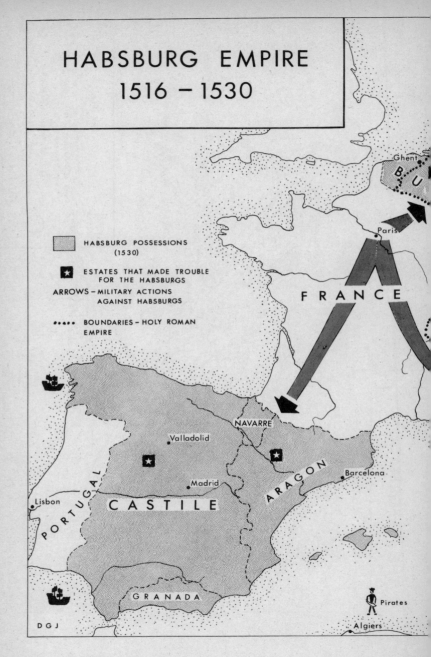

HABSBURG EMPIRE
1516 – 1530

Ghent

B U

Paris

HABSBURG POSSESSIONS
(1530)

ESTATES THAT MADE TROUBLE
FOR THE HABSBURGS

ARROWS – MILITARY ACTIONS
AGAINST HABSBURGS

•••• BOUNDARIES – HOLY ROMAN
EMPIRE

FRANCE

NAVARRE

Valladolid

Barcelona

Madrid

ARAGON

Lisbon

PORTUGAL

CASTILE

GRANADA

Pirates

DGJ

Algiers

Ottoman Conquests
1514 – 1600

- Vienna
- Mohács (1526)
- Venice
- Belgrade (1521)
- Rome
- Algiers (1556)
- Tunis (1574)
- Tripoli (1551)

Ottoman Lands and Tributaries:

c.1514

c.1600

0   200
M i l e

Istanbul

Cyprus
(1573)

Damascus
(1516)

Tabriz

Shiah Revolt
early 16th century

Isfahan

Baghdad
(1534, 1555)

Cairo
(1517)

Mecca
(1517)

DGJ

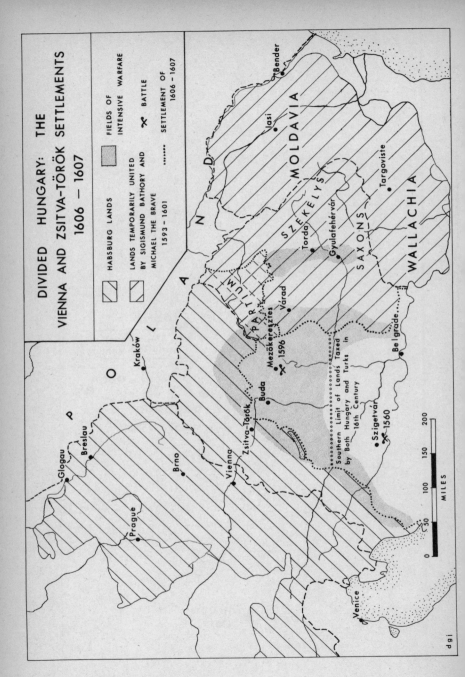

DIVIDED HUNGARY: THE VIENNA AND ZSITVA-TÖRÖK SETTLEMENTS 1606 – 1607

HABSBURG LANDS

LANDS TEMPORARILY UNITED BY SIGISMUND BÁTHORY AND MICHAEL THE BRAVE 1593 – 1601

FIELDS OF INTENSIVE WARFARE

✗ BATTLE

SETTLEMENT OF 1606 – 1607

Bender

Iasi

MOLDAVIA

Targoviste

SZEKELYS

Gyulafehérvár

SAXONS

WALLACHIA

Torda

P A R T I U M

Várad

Mezőkeresztes ✗ 1596

Belgrade

Buda

Szigetvár ✗ 1560

Zsitva-Török

Southern Limit of Lands Taxed by Both Hungary and Turks in 16th Century

Vienna

P O L A N D

Kraków

Breslau

Glogau

Brno

Prague

Venice

0   50   100   150   200

MILES

jgp

84 /   MAP 35

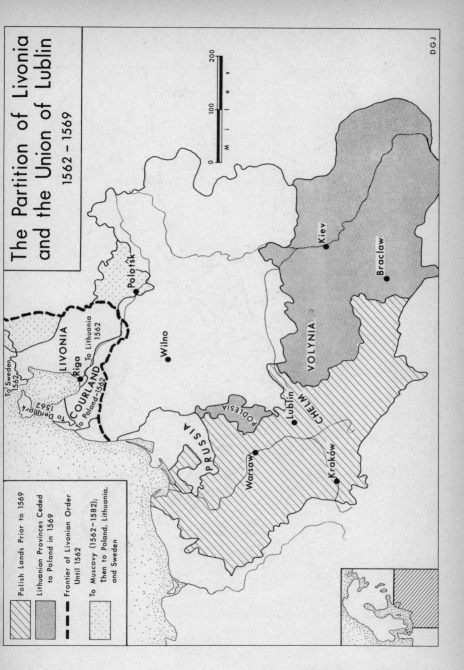

The Partition of Livonia
and the Union of Lublin
1562 - 1569

0   100   200
Miles

DGJ

Polotsk
Wilno
Riga
To Sweden 1562
LIVONIA
To Lithuania 1562
COURLAND
To Poland 1562
To Denmark 1562
Kiev
Braclaw
VOLYNIA
Lublin
CHELM
PODLESIA
PRUSSIA
Warsaw
Kraków

Polish Lands Prior to 1569

Lithuanian Provinces Ceded
to Poland in 1569

Frontier of Livonian Order
Until 1562

To Muscovy (1562–1582);
then to Poland, Lithuania,
and Sweden

MAP 36   / 85

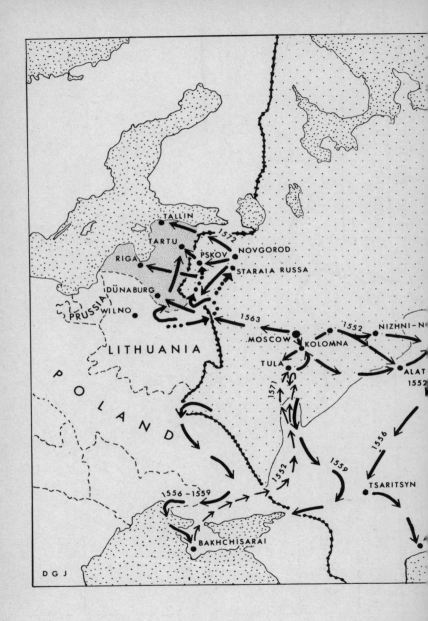

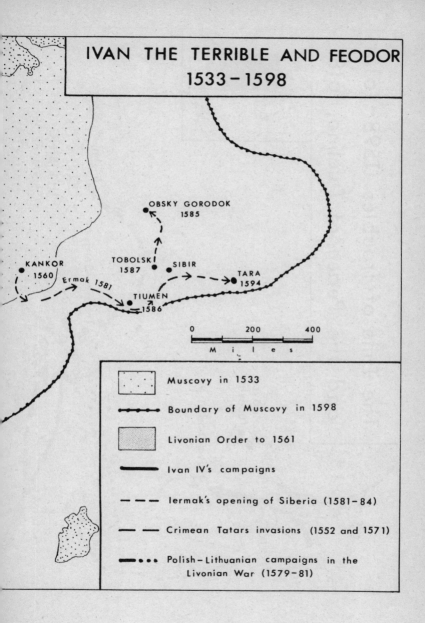

IVAN THE TERRIBLE AND FEODOR
1533 – 1598

OBSKY GORODOK
1585

KANKOR
1560

TOBOLSK
1587

SIBIR

TARA
1594

Ermak 1581

TIUMEN
1586

0   200   400

M i l e s

Muscovy in 1533

Boundary of Muscovy in 1598

Livonian Order to 1561

Ivan IV's campaigns

Iermak's opening of Siberia (1581–84)

Crimean Tatars invasions (1552 and 1571)

Polish–Lithuanian campaigns in the
Livonian War (1579–81)

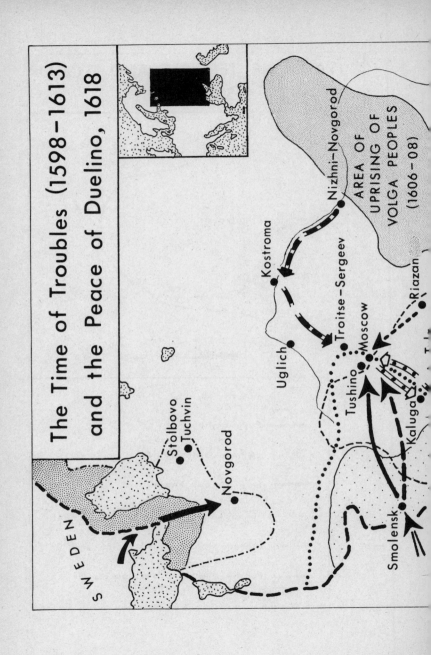

The Time of Troubles (1598–1613) and the Peace of Duelino, 1618

AREA OF UPRISING OF VOLGA PEOPLES (1606–08)

Nizhni–Novgorod

Kostroma

Troitse–Sergeev

Uglich

Moscow

Tushino

Riazan

Kaluga

Stolbovo
Tuchvin

Novgorod

S W E D E N

Smolensk

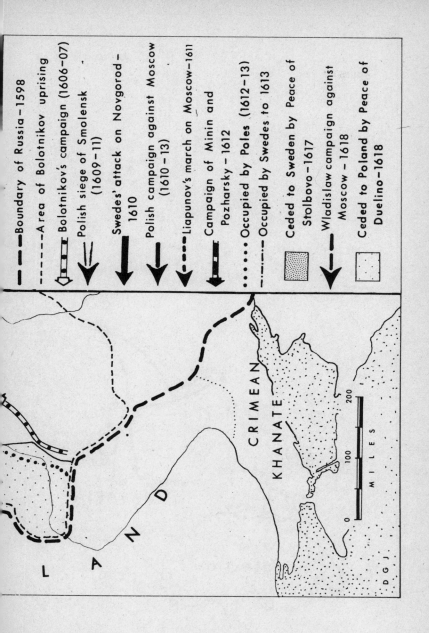

Boundary of Russia—1598

Area of Bolotnikov uprising

Bolotnikov's campaign (1606–07)

Polish siege of Smolensk (1609–11)

Swedes' attack on Novgorod—1610

Polish campaign against Moscow (1610–13)

Liapunov's march on Moscow—1611

Campaign of Minin and Pozharsky—1612

Occupied by Poles (1612–13)

Occupied by Swedes to 1613

Ceded to Sweden by Peace of Stolbovo—1617

Wladislaw campaign against Moscow—1618

Ceded to Poland by Peace of Duelino—1618

CRIMEAN

KHANATE

MILES

0   100   200

L A N D

D G J

DENMARK

1627

Wallenstein

Lübeck

SW.

SW.
1628

SW.

UNITED
NETHERLANDS

Osnabrück

BRANDEN

Stadtlohn
1623

Münster

Magdeburg

Dessau
1626

Breitenfeld

Wal

Mansfeld

1631

Lutzen
1632

Gustavus Adolphus

Frankfurt

1632

Wh

1620

1632

PALATINATE

FR.

1622

FR.

Wallenstein

BOH

FR.

Nördlingen
1634

Breisach

Augsburg

Regensburg

L

FR.

BAVARIA

Salzburg

SWISS

CONFEDERATION

Valtellina R.

Milan

VENICE

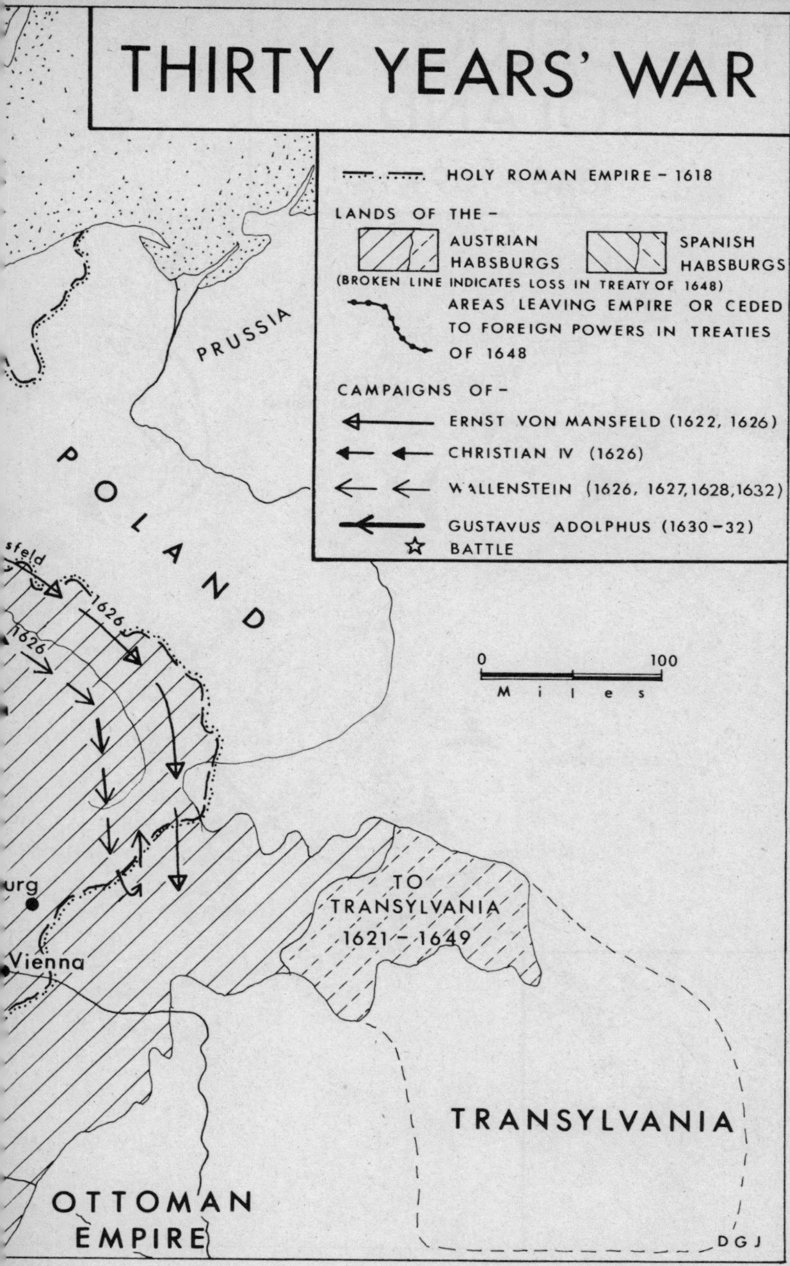

THIRTY YEARS' WAR

.... HOLY ROMAN EMPIRE - 1618

LANDS OF THE -

AUSTRIAN HABSBURGS   SPANISH HABSBURGS

(BROKEN LINE INDICATES LOSS IN TREATY OF 1648)

AREAS LEAVING EMPIRE OR CEDED TO FOREIGN POWERS IN TREATIES OF 1648

CAMPAIGNS OF -

ERNST VON MANSFELD (1622, 1626)

CHRISTIAN IV (1626)

WALLENSTEIN (1626, 1627, 1628, 1632)

GUSTAVUS ADOLPHUS (1630-32)

☆ BATTLE

0   100

M i l e s

PRUSSIA

P O L A N D

...sfeld

1626

1626

...urg

Vienna

TO TRANSYLVANIA 1621 - 1649

TRANSYLVANIA

OTTOMAN EMPIRE

DGJ

THE DELUGE IN POLAND
1648–1699

LIVONI

Riga
(Swedish
1621)

1655

Kowno

Königsberg
Oliva
Danzig
PRUSSIA
(INDEPENDENT
1654)

Wilno
Sept. 1655
1655

POMERANIA
July
1655

1655

No

Aug. 1655
1657
1655

Warsaw
Brest
1655

1656
1658-57
1655
Lublin

SILESIA
Czestochowa
1655
Zamość
(Nov. 1648)

Kraków
Beresteczk
1651

Lwów
Zborów
(Aug. 1649)

Zurawno
Buczacz

MOLDAVI

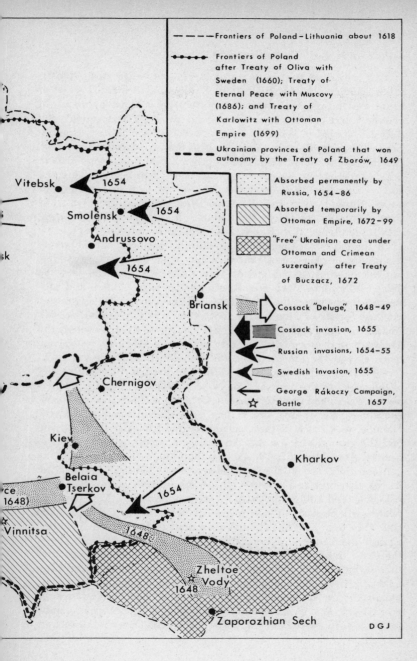

Frontiers of Poland–Lithuania about 1618

Frontiers of Poland after Treaty of Oliva with Sweden (1660); Treaty of Eternal Peace with Muscovy (1686); and Treaty of Karlowitz with Ottoman Empire (1699)

Ukrainian provinces of Poland that won autonomy by the Treaty of Zborów, 1649

Absorbed permanently by Russia, 1654–86

Absorbed temporarily by Ottoman Empire, 1672–99

"Free" Ukrainian area under Ottoman and Crimean suzerainty after Treaty of Buczacz, 1672

Cossack "Deluge", 1648–49

Cossack invasion, 1655

Russian invasions, 1654–55

Swedish invasion, 1655

George Rákoczy Campaign, 1657
☆ Battle

Vitebsk

1654

Smolensk

1654

Andrussovo

1654

Briansk

Chernigov

Kiev

Kharkov

Belaia Tserkov

1654

ce 1648)

Vinnitsa

1648

Zheltoe Vody

1648

Zaporozhian Sech

DGJ

93

Colonization and Westernization (Maps 41–52)

Two important concomitants of the Western European Renaissance significantly affected Eastern Europe and Russia. The first of these was the physical expansion of Western Europe by means of conquest and colonization. The second was "Westernization"—the diffusion abroad of Western ideas and technology. Initially, the nations of Eastern Europe participated in the expansion of the West. But during the seventeenth and eighteenth centuries, some of them became victims of expansionism and were themselves subjugated and colonized by Western powers. All of the East European lands passed through successive phases of Westernization; in effect, they were culturally colonized. But though all were deeply influenced, they responded to this often painful process in different ways.

Of the eastern nations, Russia made the greatest contribution to the physical expansion of Europe. Even while Muscovy was suffering the internal convulsions of Ivan the Terrible's reign and the Time of Troubles (*Map 38*), Russian trappers, explorers, and missionaries penetrated the Ural highlands and carried Russian power into the forests of Siberia. By 1689, they had established Russia's frontier on the Pacific (*Maps 41, 44*). On the southern frontier, the Treaty of Andrusovo with Poland (1667) gave Moscow the Cossack lands east of the Dnepr (*Map 40*). Subsequently, Peter the Great (1689–1725) and Catherine II (1762–96) pressed Russia's frontier to the coasts of the Azov and Black seas (*Maps 42, 43, 47*). Catherine even dreamed of absorbing the Ottoman Empire; her grandson, Alexander I (1801–25), drove the Turks beyond the Prut and the Danube, won much of the Caucasus region from the Persians, and laid the groundwork for Russian nineteenth-century imperialism in Central Asia (*Maps 52, 53; see also 62, 63*).

Meanwhile, the intellectual colonization of Russia commenced. In the sixteenth and seventeenth centuries, certain military, technological, and cultural innovations were imported by Muscovy; but while early Russian "Westernizers" were tempted to increase the flow, they were held back by the obscurantist Church, which warned against the dangers of heretical knowledge (*Maps 31, 32*). Peter the Great did his best to change this situation in a short period of time (*Map 42*). After visiting Holland, Germany, Austria, and England (1697–98), he cast obscurantism aside. Vigorously, if unsystematically, he set himself to the work of building a Western-style army, navy, and government. He built a modern European capital for Russia (St. Petersburg—*Map 73*), tried to educate the aristocracy along German and French lines, and sought to give Russia a modern industrial and commercial base. But his demands for money, labor, and soldiers, and his habit of assigning peasants to personal favorites and industrial concessionaires, actually expanded the institution of serfdom. He thus worsened the profound social tensions that had provoked dangerous peasant and Cossack uprisings like that of Stenka Razin in the late seventeenth century (*Map 41, inset*). His own reign was marked by violent rebellions violently suppressed; even fifty years after his death, Empress Catherine the Great was hard pressed by the rebellion of the Cossack Pugachev (*Maps 42, 45*). But though Peter did not solve the fundamental social problem of serfdom, he laid the groundwork for the swiftly expanding "Westernization" that continued throughout the eighteenth century. Perhaps it is symbolic that Catherine the Great was a German who wrote in French. Russia had become a cultural "colony" of Western Europe.

Of all the lands in Eastern Europe, the Balkans contributed least to European expansion, and, to a greater degree than any other part of Eastern Europe, they became colonial territories of the West. Unlike Russia, the Ottoman Empire in the sixteenth and seventeenth centuries rejected Western technical innovations as well as the West's religion and culture. The immediate consequence of this rejection was a precipitous decline in Ottoman power (*Maps 46, 47*). In 1683, the failure of a Turkish siege of Vienna led to the loss of Hungary. By the treaties of Karlowitz (1699) and Passarowitz (1718), Istanbul recognized the extension of European power into Dalmatia, the Greek lands, Serbia, and Wallachia. By the Treaty of Kuchuk-Kainardji (1774), Istanbul conceded to Russia the entire northern coast of the Black Sea, including Moslem Crimea, and accepted Russia's right to "protect" the Romanian principalities and all Christians under Ottoman rule. Other treaties (the "Capitulations") gave special privileges to British and French and other Western Europeans within the Ottoman realm. By the late eighteenth century, these concessions of privilege, combined with the economic stagnation resulting from Ottoman policies, had opened the entire Empire to European commercial exploitation.

Western Europeans were so deeply impressed by the backwardness of the Turks that they came to regard even the Christians in the Balkans as inferior. After 1683, for example, the Habsburgs encouraged the Orthodox Serbs and Romanians to revolt against the Turks, but no sooner had Habsburg armies moved into Serbia to help than they broke their promise of religious tolerance and initiated a vigorous campaign of catholicization; in 1739, when the

Habsburgs ran into political difficulties, they had no hesitation about handing both Serbian and Romanian lands back to the Turks in order to win peace. Similarly, the Russians in 1770 encouraged the Christian Greeks to overthrow the Ottoman yoke, but in the peace negotiations that followed, they largely overlooked Greek interests and left the rebels to the mercies of the Turks (*Maps 47, 52*).

In Central Europe, both participation in the expansion of Europe and subjugation to European colonization assumed more subtle forms than in Russia and the Balkans. The Habsburg polity of Austria, Bohemia, and Hungary was, like Russia, on the Western frontier. It is often said that late in the seventeenth century this fragile personal union of Western and Eastern European lands contributed substantially to the expansion of Europe by driving the Turks out of Hungary and back from the Danube into Serbia and Wallachia (*Map 46*). Subsequently, Austria expanded Europe, in the sense that it resettled the Pannonian Plain, virtually a virgin steppe after one hundred and seventy-five years of warfare. But in reality, Austria's contribution to the expansion of Europe consisted largely in the reconquest and colonization of the eastern Habsburg possessions (*Map 48*). After it had "liberated" Hungary from the Turks (*Map 46*), Austria sent German administrators and Roman Catholic missionaries into the Calvinist Hungarian lands. In an effort to subdue Magyar strivings for independence, Vienna also systematically planted non-Magyar colonies in Pannonia. So that its "civilizing" control might remain strong, it kept Croatia, Transylvania, and a huge "Military Frontier" zone administratively separate from Hungary. In sum, the Austrian polity contributed, as did Russia, to the expansion of Europe; but unlike Russia, the eastern Habsburg lands suffered a European colonization comparable to that which took place in the Balkans.

Northeastern Europe—the Prussian lands and Poland-Lithuania—considered themselves to be frontier lands of Western Europe during the Renaissance. Prussia, however, was surrounded by European states, and Poland-Lithuania was too weak after 1648 to assist in the colonization of areas outside Europe (*Maps 49, 40*). In the Northeast, the expansion of the West assumed the form of colonization within Europe. The Westernized powers here simply absorbed the "backward" lands around them.

The first partition of Poland was initiated in 1768 when a Prusso-Russian convention for the protection of religious minorities in Poland provoked a Polish religious uprising (*Map 50*). Russia and Prussia intervened and, in 1772, struck a three-way bargain with Austria whereby each acquired Polish territory. The Poles tolerated this outrage until 1790. Then, inspired by the French Revolution, they took advantage of a Russo-Turkish war to reform their constitution. Taking this reform as evidence that the "backward" Poles were incapable of self-government, the Russians and Prussians instituted a new two-way partition in 1793. When Poland rebelled, Austria was induced to help remove the once-great commonwealth from the map altogether in 1795.

Perhaps the final and most extensive act of Western Europe's expansion into Eastern Europe and Russia before the twentieth century was Napoleon's invasion (*Map 51*). In reality, Napoleon was far less interested in Eastern Europe than in France's immediate neighbors, Germany, Italy, and Spain, but his imperialism brought the benefits of modern government and French culture to the East. A full century before the emergence of a new Poland and a Yugoslavia—a union of the Southern Slavs—Napoleon pointed the way by creating a grand duchy at Warsaw and a province named Illyria in Croatia. He drove the Habsburgs and Prussia to new reforms. His wars penetrated the Islamic world, bringing about the first extensive contacts in centuries between the lethargic Ottoman ruling class and the West. Finally, Napoleon brought Western Europe, in the form of a conquering army, into Russia. To drive him out and defeat him, Russian forces pursued him to Paris and beyond (*Map 52*). This experience gave new impetus to Russia's Westernization.

THE EXPANSION OF RUS
IN THE 17th CENTURY

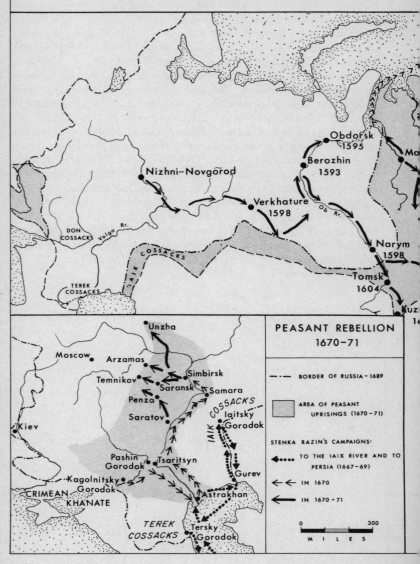

Obdofsk
1595

Berozhin
1593

Mo

Nizhni-Novgorod

Verkhature
1598

Ob Rr.

DON
COSSACKS *volga Rr.*

COSSACKS

IAIK

TEREK
COSSACKS

Narym
1598

Tomsk
1604

Kuz

PEASANT REBELLION
1670-71

Unzha

Moscow   Arzamas

Temnikov   Simbirsk
         Saransk   Samara

Penza

Saratov   Iaitsky
         Gorodok

Kiev

COSSACKS

IAIK

Pashin
Gorodok   Tsaritsyn

Kagolnitsky   Gurev
Gorodok

CRIMEAN   Astrakhan
KHANATE

*TEREK
COSSACKS*   Tersky
         Gorodok

BORDER OF RUSSIA - 1689

AREA OF PEASANT
UPRISINGS (1670-71)

STENKA RAZIN'S CAMPAIGNS:

TO THE IAIK RIVER AND TO
PERSIA (1667-69)

IN 1670

IN 1670-71

0   300
MILES

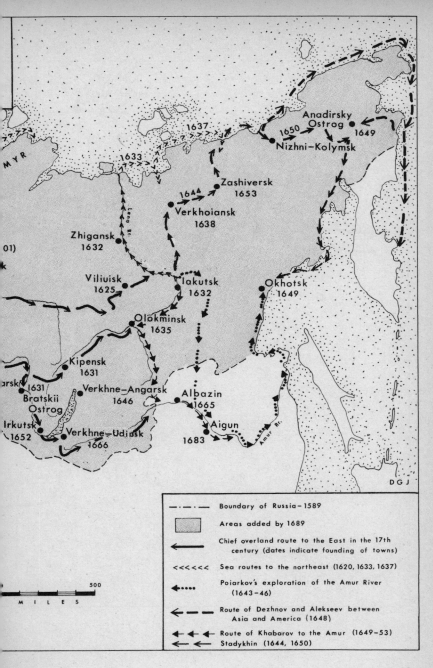

MYR

1637

1633

Anadirsky
Ostrog
1649

1650

Nizhni-Kolymsk

Zashiversk
1653

1644

Verkhoiansk
1638

Zhigansk
1632

01)

Okhotsk
1649

Viluisk
1625

Iakutsk
1632

Olokminsk
1635

Lena R.

Kipensk
1631

arsk
1631

Verkhne–Angarsk
1646

Albazin
1665

Bratskii
Ostrog

Aigun

Irkutsk
1652

Verkhne–Udinsk
1666

1683

Amur R.

D G J

Boundary of Russia – 1589

Areas added by 1689

Chief overland route to the East in the 17th
century (dates indicate founding of towns)

<<<<<< Sea routes to the northeast (1620, 1633, 1637)

••••• Poiarkov's exploration of the Amur River
(1643–46)

– – Route of Dezhnov and Alekseev between
Asia and America (1648)

Route of Khabarov to the Amur (1649–53)

Stadykhin (1644, 1650)

500

M I L E S

99

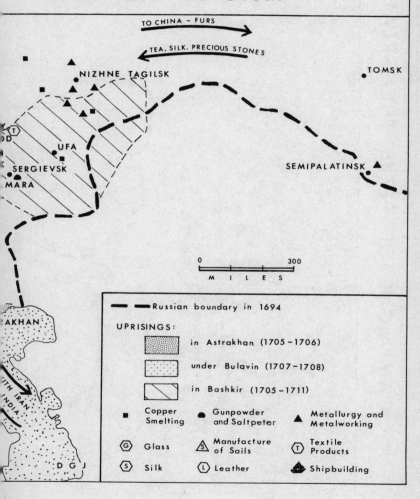

TO CHINA – FURS

TEA, SILK, PRECIOUS STONES

TOMSK

NIZHNE TAGILSK

UFA

SERGIEVSK

MARA

SEMIPALATINSK

0   300
M I L E S

AKHAN

ITH IRAN
INDIA

D G J

---Russian boundary in 1694

UPRISINGS:

in Astrakhan (1705–1706)

under Bulavin (1707–1708)

in Bashkir (1705–1711)

■ Copper Smelting

● Gunpowder and Saltpeter

▲ Metallurgy and Metalworking

Ⓖ Glass

Ⓢ Manufacture of Sails

Ⓣ Textile Products

Ⓢ Silk

Ⓛ Leather

Shipbuilding

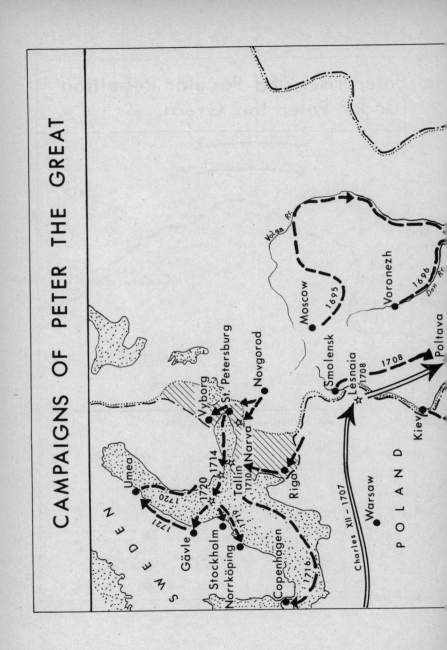

CAMPAIGNS OF PETER THE GREAT

Umeå

S W E D E N

Gävle

Stockholm

Norrköping

Vyborg

St. Petersburg

Novgorod

Narva

Tallinn

Riga

Copenhagen

1714

1720

1720

1721

1719

1710

1716

Volga R.

Moscow

1695

Smolensk

Lesnaia

1708

1708

Voronezh

1696

Don R.

Poltava

Kiev

Charles XII – 1707

Warsaw

P O L A N D

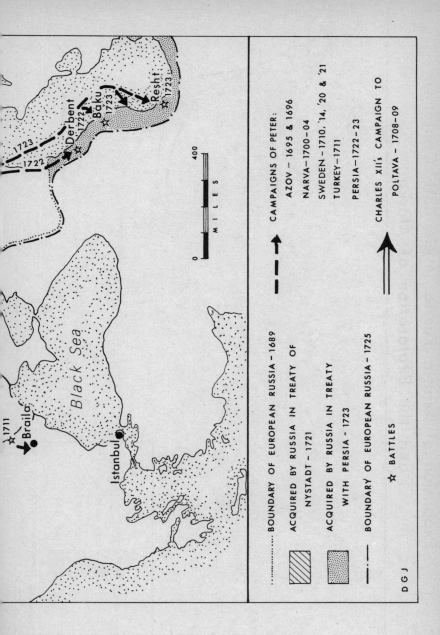

Black Sea

Istanbul

Braila
1711

Derbent
1722
Baku
1723
Resht
1723

1723
1722

MILES
0   400

BOUNDARY OF EUROPEAN RUSSIA – 1689

ACQUIRED BY RUSSIA IN TREATY OF
NYSTADT – 1721

ACQUIRED BY RUSSIA IN TREATY
WITH PERSIA – 1723

BOUNDARY OF EUROPEAN RUSSIA – 1725

☆ BATTLES

CAMPAIGNS OF PETER:

AZOV – 1695 & 1696
NARVA – 1700–04
SWEDEN – 1710, '14, '20 & '21
TURKEY – 1711
PERSIA – 1722–23

CHARLES XII's CAMPAIGN TO
POLTAVA – 1708–09

D G J

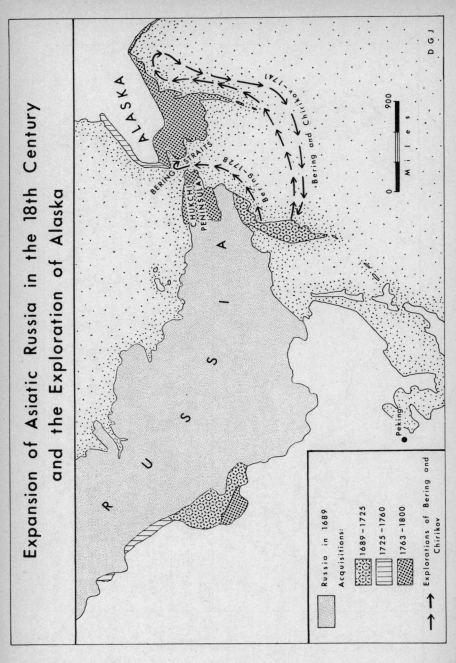

Expansion of Asiatic Russia in the 18th Century and the Exploration of Alaska

ALASKA

Bering and Chirikov - 1741

Bering - 1728

BERING STRAITS

CHUKCHI PENINSULA

R U S S I A

Peking

Russia in 1689

Acquisitions:

1689 - 1725

1725 - 1760

1763 - 1800

Explorations of Bering and Chirikov

Miles

0   900

D G J

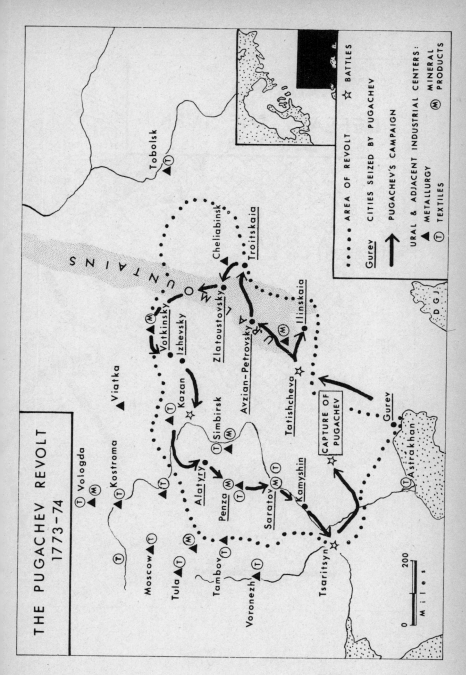

THE PUGACHEV REVOLT
1773-74

Vologda Ⓣ
Ⓜ
Kostroma ▲
Viatka ▲
Ⓣ
Moscow ▲Ⓣ
Ⓜ
Tula ▲Ⓣ
Tambov ▲Ⓣ
Voronezh Ⓣ

Tobolsk
▲Ⓣ

U R A L   M O U N T A I N S

Votkinsk Ⓜ
▲
Izhevsky
Cheliabinsk ▲
Zlatoustovsky ▲
Troitskaia
Avzian–Petrovsky ▲
Ⓜ
Ilinskaia ●
Kazan
Ⓣ
Simbirsk
Ⓜ
Alatyry ●Ⓣ ▲
Penza Ⓜ
Ⓣ
Saratov Ⓜ Ⓣ
Kamyshin ●
Tatishcheva ☆
CAPTURE OF PUGACHEV
Gurey ●
Astrakhan
Ⓣ
Tsaritsyn ☆

D G J

0   200
Miles

☆ BATTLES

••••• AREA OF REVOLT

Gurey CITIES SEIZED BY PUGACHEV

⟶ PUGACHEV'S CAMPAIGN

URAL & ADJACENT INDUSTRIAL CENTERS:

▲ METALLURGY   Ⓜ MINERAL
                              PRODUCTS

Ⓣ TEXTILES

MAP 45   /105

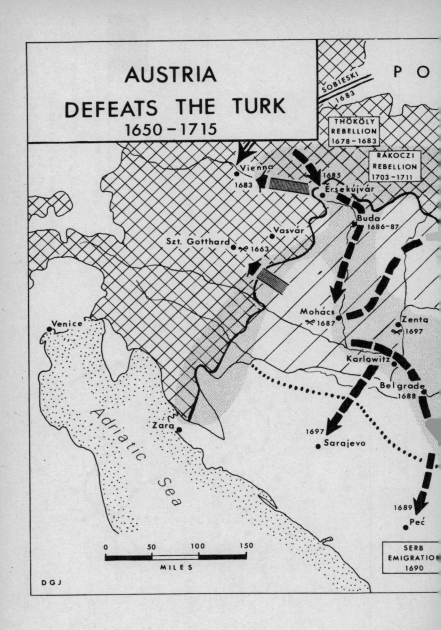

AUSTRIA
DEFEATS THE TURK
1650–1715

P O

SOBIESKI
1683

THÖKÖLY
REBELLION
1678–1683

RÁKOCZI
REBELLION
1703–1711

Vienna
1683

1685
Érsekújvár

Buda
1686–87

Vasvár

Szt. Gotthard ✕ 1663

Mohács
✕ 1687

Zenta
✕ 1697

Venice

Karlowitz

Belgrade
1688

Zara

1697
Sarajevo

Adriatic

Sea

1689
Peć

SERB
EMIGRATION
1690

0   50   100   150

MILES

DGJ

N D

P O D O L I A

Zurawno

Buczacz

✂ 1672

Kameniec

Chocim

Szatmar

SOBIESKI'S
DISASTER – 1686

M O L D A V I A

lasi

Nagyvárad

660

1687

Akkerman

R A N S Y L V A N I A

1658-62

ár

Kronstadt

1690

Black Sea

WALLACHIA

itz

OLTENIA

Vidin

iš

1689

Sofia

Legend

⊠ HABSBURG LANDS
1683

LANDS LAID
WASTE
1658 – 1718

╱ LANDS GAINED BY HABSBURGS AT KARLOWITZ
(KARLOVCI) – 1699

•••• FRONTIER GAINED AT PASSAROWITZ
(POŽAROVÁC) – 1718, BUT LOST AT
BELGRADE – 1739

▦➤ TURK OFFENSIVES (1658-83)

➤ IMPERIAL OFFENSIVES (1683-99)

✂ BATTLE

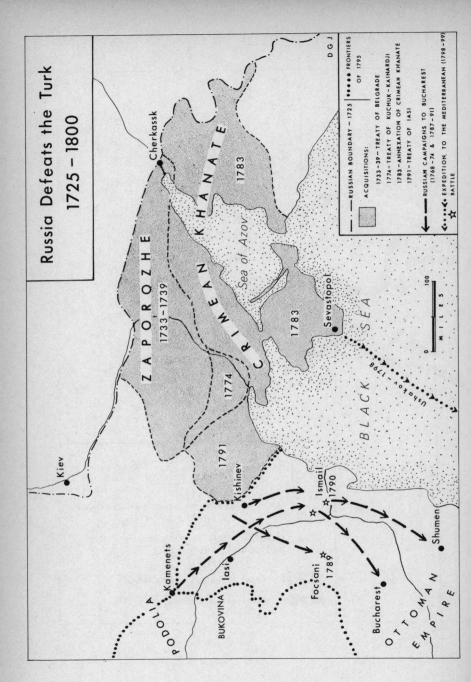

Russia Defeats the Turk
1725-1800

RUSSIAN BOUNDARY — 1725

•••• FRONTIERS OF 1795

ACQUISITIONS:
1733-39 — TREATY OF BELGRADE
1774 — TREATY OF KUCHUK-KAINARDJI
1783 — ANNEXATION OF CRIMEAN KHANATE
1791 — TREATY OF IASI

RUSSIAN CAMPAIGNS TO BUCHAREST (1768-74 & 1787-91)

•••• EXPEDITION TO THE MEDITERRANEAN (1798-99)
☆ BATTLE

Cherkassk

ZAPOROZHE

1733-1739

CRIMEAN KHANATE

1783

Sea of Azov

1783

Sevastopol

1774

BLACK SEA

Ushakov-1798

Kiev

1791

Kishinev

0   100
MILES

Kamenets

Ismail
1790
☆

Iasi

BUKOVINA

Focsani
1789 ☆

Shumen

PODOLIA

Bucharest

OTTOMAN

EMPIRE

DGJ

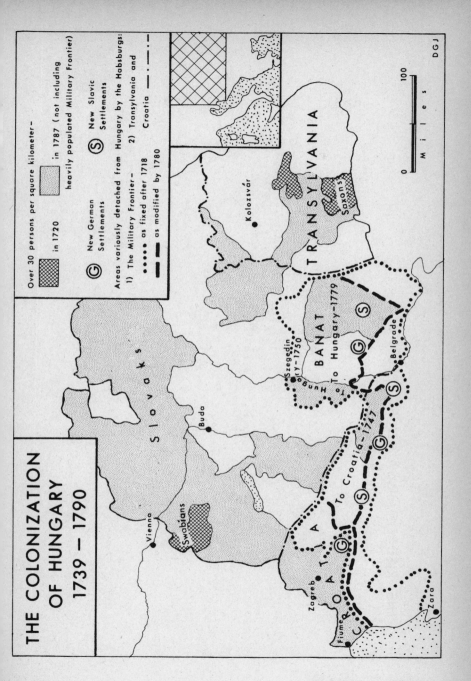

THE COLONIZATION
OF HUNGARY
1739 – 1790

Over 30 persons per square kilometer—

in 1720

in 1787 (not including
heavily populated Military Frontier)

Ⓖ New German
Settlements

Ⓢ New Slavic
Settlements

Areas variously detached from Hungary by the Habsburgs:

1) The Military Frontier—

•••• as fixed after 1718

━━ as modified by 1780

2) Transylvania and
Croatia —••—••—

TRANSYLVANIA

Saxons

Kolozsvár

Slovaks

Swabians

Vienna

Buda

Zagreb

Fiume

Zara

Belgrade

Szegedin

To Hungary–1779

To Croatia–1747

BANAT

Ⓢ

Ⓖ

Ⓢ

Ⓖ

Ⓢ

Ⓖ

DGJ

Miles

0   100

MAP 48   /109

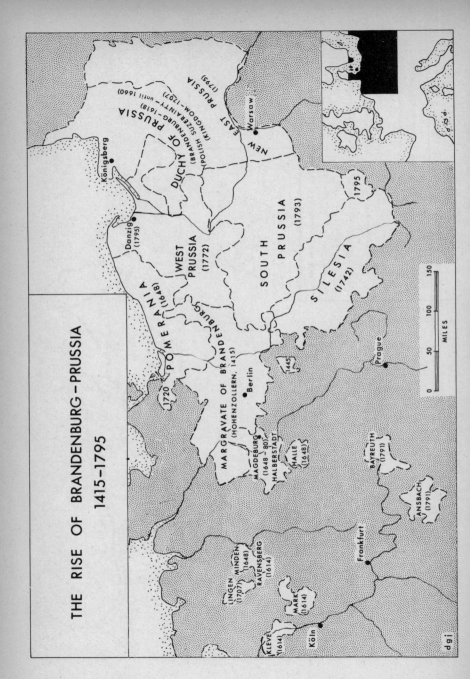

THE RISE OF BRANDENBURG–PRUSSIA
1415–1795

EAST PRUSSIA (1795)

DUCHY OF PRUSSIA
(BRANDENBURG–1618)
(POLISH SUZERAINTY – until 1660)
(KINGDOM – 1701)

NEW

Warsaw

Königsberg

Danzig (1795)

WEST PRUSSIA (1772)

SOUTH PRUSSIA (1793)

1795

SILESIA (1742)

POMERANIA (1648)

MARGRAVATE OF BRANDENBURG (HOHENZOLLERN, 1415)

1720

Berlin

1445

Prague

MAGDEBURG (1648–801)

HALBERSTADT

HALLE (1648)

BAYREUTH (1791)

ANSBACH (1791)

INGEN (1707)

MINDEN (1648)

RAVENSBERG (1614)

MARK (1614)

KLEVE (1614)

Köln

Frankfurt

MILES

0   50   100   150

lgi

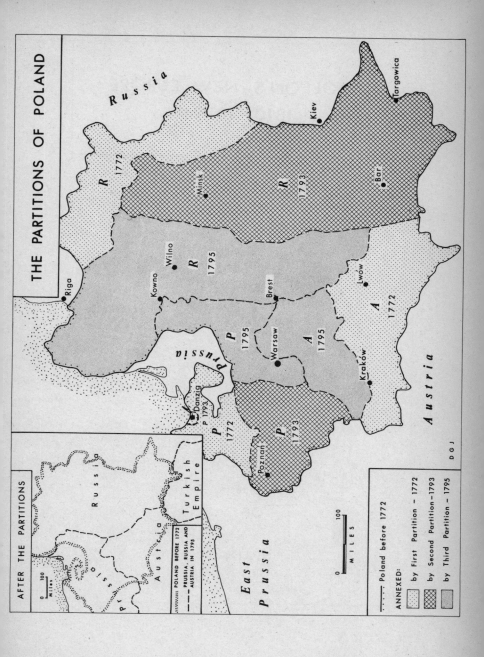

THE PARTITIONS OF POLAND

Russia

Kiev

Targowica

R 1772

Riga

R 1793

Minsk

Bar

Wilno

R 1795

Kowno

Brest

Lwów

A 1772

P 1795

Warsaw

A 1795

Kraków

P*russia*

Danzig
P 1793

P 1772

P 1793

Poznan

East Prussia

Austria

D G J

AFTER THE PARTITIONS

Russia

Austria

Turkish Empire

Prussia

0   100
MILES

.... POLAND BEFORE 1772
— — — PRUSSIA, RUSSIA AND AUSTRIA IN 1795

ANNEXED:

..... Poland before 1772

by First Partition – 1772

by Second Partition – 1793

by Third Partition – 1795

0   100
MILES

MAP 50   /111

NAPOLEON'S NEW EUROPE
1810 – 1815

Ham

Amsterdam

London

CC

Amiens

Mayence

Paris

SW
CONFE

Bordeaux

Mila

Marengo

Toulon

KINGDOM

Madrid

OF

SPAIN

| 0 | 100 | 200 |
MILES

dgi

Stockholm

Moscow

Borodino

Copenhagen

Smolensk

Tilsit

Friedland

GRAND DUCHY

OF

WARSAW

(1807–1813)

Berlin

ATION

Jena

Erfurt

Austerlitz

Pressburg

Vienna

AUSTRIAN

Iasi

3)

Hohenlinden

EMPIRE

(1804)

ILLYRIA

1809–1813

Campo

Formio

Bucharest

A.

ALY

–1813)

Ragusa

Istanbul

Rome

KGDM.

OF

NAPLES

(1806–1813)

LANDS INCORPORATED INTO
REVOLUTIONARY FRANCE

LANDS REORGANIZED WITHOUT
INCORPORATION INTO FRANCE

NAPOLEON'S RUSSIAN CAMPAIGN

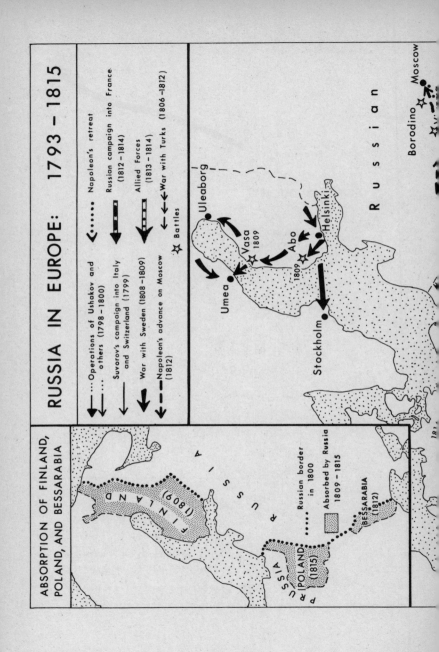

RUSSIA IN EUROPE: 1793 – 1815

····· Operations of Ushakov and others (1798–1800)

↓ Suvorov's campaign into Italy and Switzerland (1799)

↓ War with Sweden (1808–1809)

⇠ Napoleon's advance on Moscow (1812)

◦◦◦◦ Napoleon's retreat

↓ Russian campaign into France (1812–1814)

↓ Allied Forces (1813–1814)

←↞ War with Turks (1806–1812)

☆ Battles

ABSORPTION OF FINLAND, POLAND, AND BESSARABIA

····· Russian border in 1800

▦ Absorbed by Russia 1809–1815

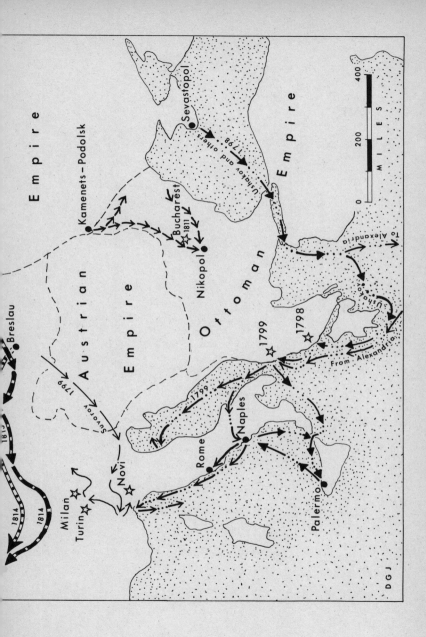

Part IV

The Nineteenth Century After Napoleon

During the three-quarters of a century following Napoleon's fall, Eastern Europe and Russia Westernized and modernized themselves with revolutionary swiftness. To a considerable extent, the era of their backwardness was ended. However, they remained politically bound and culturally subordinated to the West, and these involvements hindered their efforts to shake off the bonds of the past.

Many of the nations of Eastern Europe gained some form of independence during this period. Between 1804 and 1833, the Serbs won the Ottoman sultan's reluctant recognition of their autonomy within his realm (*Map 54*). Between 1821 and 1832, the Greeks revolted and obtained full independence. In 1848, the Italians, Germans, Hungarians, Habsburg Slavs, and Romanians all manifested their desires for national statehood in a great wave of revolutions—all of which failed (*Maps 56, 57*). But in the following years, the Romanians won unity (1859) and virtual independence (1866) (*Maps 55, 58*), while in the West, a national Italy emerged in 1859. New constitutional arrangements in Austria gave Hungary broad autonomy in 1867, and a new German Empire was established in 1871 (*Map 58*). By then, the moment was not far away when a Congress of the Powers at Berlin (1878) would recreate Bulgaria and finally free the Serbs and Romanians from Ottoman rule (*Map 60*).

Meanwhile, personal emancipation was proceeding. Prussia passed legislation against serfdom during the Napoleonic period. Between 1816 and 1819, the serfs were freed in the Baltic lands belonging to Russia. In the 1830's, the revolutionary Sultan Mahmud II (1808–39) abolished several forms of feudalism in his Empire. The Habsburgs ceded personal liberty to the serfs throughout their lands during the revolution of 1848; in 1861, Tsar Alexander II (1855–81) liberated the serfs of Russia; and Romania abolished serfdom in 1864. In different degrees, Greece, Serbia, and Bulgaria eliminated serfdom and expropriated the lands of the feudal classes at the moments of their national liberations.

Urban growth, the beginnings of industrialization, and the spread of education also contributed to the liberation of Eastern Europe and Russia from the bonds of the past. Between 1800 and 1880, Moscow more than doubled its size. Warsaw and Prague grew threefold; St. Petersburg, fourfold; Vienna, fivefold (*Map 59*); Budapest, sixfold; and Berlin increased its population eight times. Meanwhile, Bohemia in the Austrian lands, Saxony and Silesia in eastern Germany, St. Petersburg, Moscow, the Urals, and central Poland in Russia were all advancing into the new industrial age. Symbolic of this was the fact that by 1851, Warsaw, Prague, Berlin, Vienna, and Trieste were connected with one another and the West by rail, and a railway had been completed between St. Petersburg and Moscow (*Map 64*). As late as 1856, Istanbul lacked even telegraphic contact with Europe, but thirty years later, trains connected it with Vienna and the rest of Europe.

One of the most significant forces for change in the post-Napoleonic era was a newly educated element of society—the people whom the Russians called *intelligentsia*. Deeply influenced by Western ideas, particularly those of the French Revolution, the intelligentsia condemned the political and social systems of their nations and demanded radical reforms in the name of such grandiose principles as "justice," "equality," and "freedom." Impatient and determined, they became the inspirers and leaders of revolutions. While their intentions were good, their insistence upon using revolutionary violence to achieve their ends was highly detrimental to the smoothness and rapidity of the emancipation process. Their injurious influence is well illustrated by the revolt that broke out in Russian Poland in November, 1830 (*Map 61*). Inspired to a considerable extent by political disturbances in France, it was led, in part, by émigrés in the West. Through lack of preparation, it collapsed, succeeding only in bringing new disasters to Poland in the form of Russian reprisals.

In 1848, the commitment to international revolutionary ideals was so strong among the educated classes of Central and Eastern Europe that a new revolution in France touched off rebellions in every significant urban complex in the area (*Map 56*). Yet, as it turned out, these rebellions lacked popular support. In a few large cities, such as Vienna, the presence of urban masses produced radical social upheavals. But everywhere else—in Germany, Bohemia, Hungary, and Romania, and Italy in the West—the liberal and nationalistic bourgeoisie, having acted primarily on a signal from the West, had to backtrack before the forces of reaction, with dire consequences for the future development of their nations (*Map 57*).

While Western-inspired nationalistic revolutions led by the Eastern European intelligentsia simultaneously drove forward and complicated the processes of emancipation, other social elements, primarily conservative governing circles, stood firmly against change. After 1789, the onetime "enlightened despots" of Eastern Europe and Russia turned from revolutionary innovation inspired by Western rationalism to fear inspired by the French Revolution. Setting authority against reason, they banded together on a platform of international reaction. At the Congress of Vienna in 1815, Russia, Prussia, and Austria sought to return "legitimate" rulers to their thrones in the hope that the restored monarchs would wipe out all memory of the Revolution (*Map 53*). However, they often confused legitimacy with the "will of the victors." For instance, they accepted the destruction of hundreds of tiny states in Germany and assigned Prussia vast territories along the Rhine. They permitted the Habsburgs to exchange their far-flung Netherland and Italian provinces for lands in northern Italy and Germany. And they re-partitioned Poland, assigning most of that country to Russia. The Congress Powers assumed that the maintenance of peace and legitimacy required police measures. Austria's chancellor, Prince Metternich (1809–48), and Tsar Alexander I (1801–25) initiated an anti-revolutionary "Holy Alliance" that bound its members to guide their relations with one another according to the principles of Christian morality. Tsar Nicholas I, in 1833, transformed this alliance into a military league between Russia, Prussia, and Austria.

In its various forms, the Holy Alliance attempted to block change and emancipation in Eastern Europe throughout the nineteenth century. At first, as a police system, it lasted only a few years. The British defected in the 1820's, and the revolt of the Greeks (an Orthodox people), which began in 1821, led even the Russians to reconsider the wisdom of preventing all political change on principle. In the late 1820's, both Britain and Russia helped the Greek rebels against the Turks (*Map 54*). Nevertheless, loyalty to the Alliance kept Tsar Nicholas I from finishing off the Ottoman "sick man of Europe" in 1829–33 (*Maps 54, 55, 62*). And in 1849, after revolution had overthrown Metternich and after Prussia had decided to foster the creation of a united German state, the commitment to preserve the old order inspired Tsar Nicholas to reverse the tide of progress throughout Central Europe by sending his armies to suppress revolutionary Hungary (*Map 57*). Meanwhile, Russia had begun its eastward advance into Central Asia (*Map 63*).

The Alliance received what appeared to be its death blow in the Crimean War (1853–56), when Russia met defeat on its own territory at the hands of the British and French while Prussia and Austria stood aside (*Map 55*). In the years following the Crimean War, Prussia and Austria, the other pillars of the European Alliance, fell away. Prussia, guided by the great Chancellor Bismarck (1862–91), used revolutionary methods to achieve Germany's unification and a general reformation of the power relationships of all Europe. Meanwhile, the absolutist regime Tsar Nicholas had restored in Austria in 1849 collapsed (*Map 58*). Austria virtually ceased to be a great power; defeated by France and Italy in 1859 and by Prussia in 1866, it lost its territorial footholds in Italy and Germany. Even in Russia, the post-Crimean era witnessed a wave of significant reforms under Alexander II that violated the conservative spirit of the Holy Alliance.

Conservatism, however, was far from beaten. In 1873, Bismarck himself took the initiative in re-establishing the alliance between the three great powers of Eastern Europe. Although his alliance never opposed change as resolutely as had the old Congress System, it provided the forces of reaction in Eastern Europe with an instrument of control that was still serviceable in the first years of the twentieth century. Moreover, it helped to distort efforts to introduce change in the area by enforcing compromises with the social and political systems of the past.

The Triumph of Legitimacy
1815 – 1820

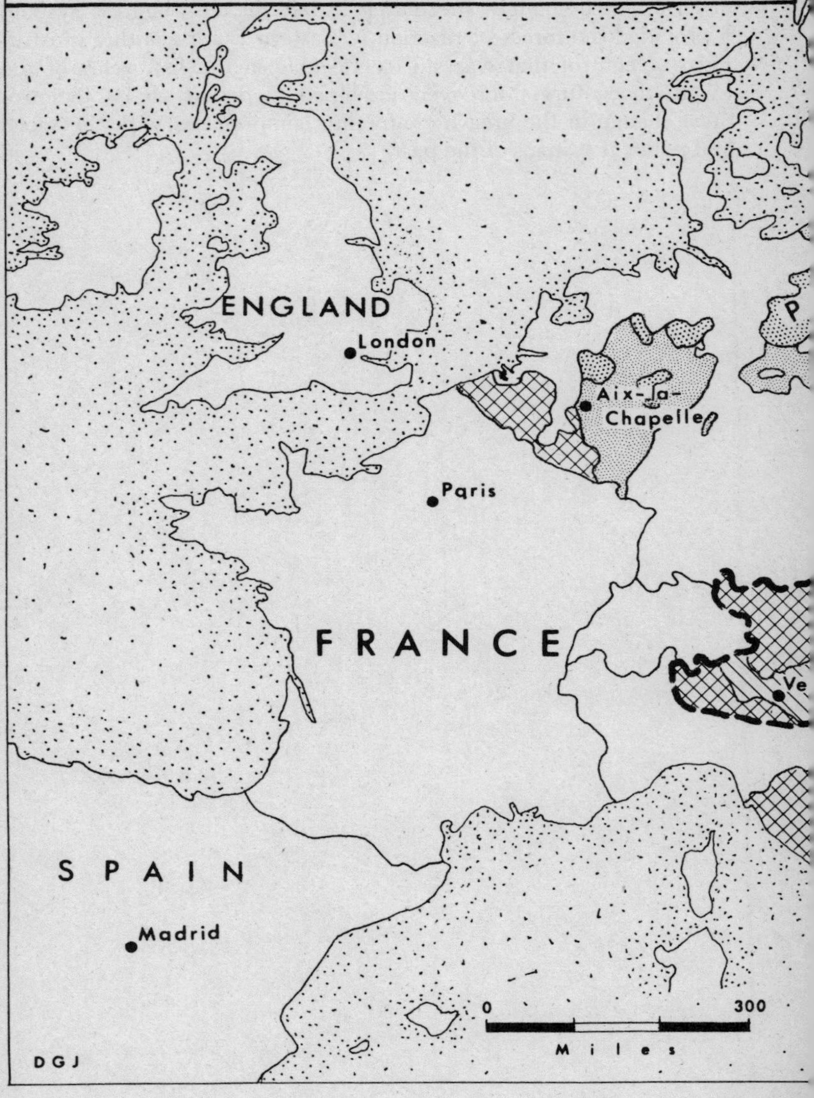

ENGLAND

London

Aix-la-
Chapelle

Paris

FRANCE

Ve

SPAIN

Madrid

0   300
M i l e s

DGJ

St. Petersburg

R U S S I A

Warsaw

Vienna

AUSTRIA

Laibach

ppau

OTTOMAN

EMPIRE

Naples

	Prussia in 1770		Added after 1815
	Russia in 1770		Added after 1770
	Habsburg lands in 1770		Added after 1770

Frontiers after 1815:

●●●●●● Russian

▬ ▬ ▬ Austrian

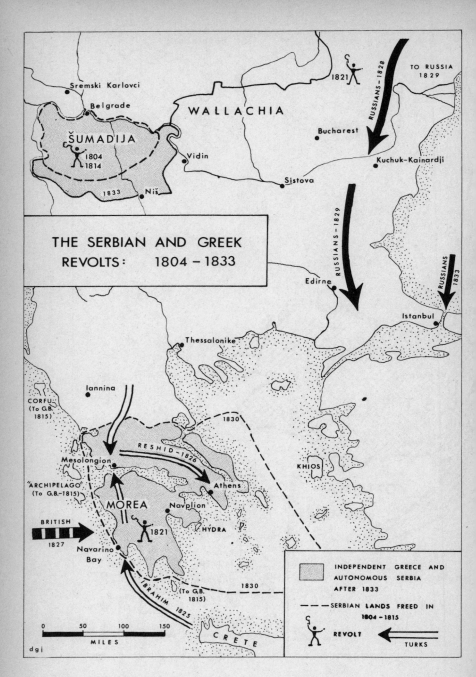

THE SERBIAN AND GREEK
REVOLTS: 1804 – 1833

Sremski Karlovci

Belgrade

ŠUMADIJA
1804
1814

1833

Niš

WALLACHIA

Vidin

Sistova

Bucharest

Kuchuk-Kainardji

1821

RUSSIANS – 1828

TO RUSSIA
1829

RUSSIANS – 1829

RUSSIANS
1833

Edirne

Istanbul

Thessalonike

Iannina

CORFU
(To G.B.
1815)

RESHID – 1826

Mesolongion

Athens

KHIOS

"ARCHIPELAGO"
(To G.B.–1815)

MOREA

Navplion

HYDRA

BRITISH
1827

Navarino
Bay

1821

IBRAHIM
1825

(To G.B.
1815)

1830

CRETE

0   50   100   150
MILES

dgi

INDEPENDENT GREECE AND
AUTONOMOUS SERBIA
AFTER 1833

SERBIAN LANDS FREED IN
1804 – 1815

REVOLT

TURKS

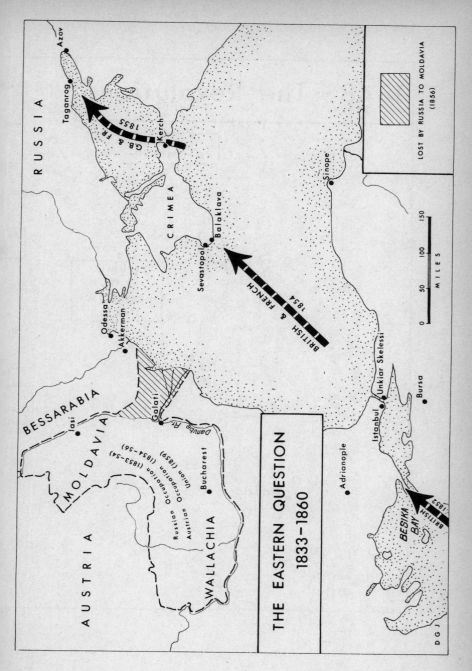

THE EASTERN QUESTION
1833–1860

LOST BY RUSSIA TO MOLDAVIA
(1856)

RUSSIA

Azov

Taganrog

Kerch

G.B. & FR. 1855

CRIMEA

Balaklava

Sevastopol

BRITISH & FRENCH 1854

Sinope

Odessa

Akkerman

BESSARABIA

Iasi

MOLDAVIA

Galati

Danube R.

Russian Occupation (1853–54)

Austrian Occupation (1854–56)

Union (1859)

Bucharest

WALLACHIA

AUSTRIA

Adrianople

Istanbul

Unkiar Skelessi

Bursa

BESIKA BAY

BRITISH 1852

MILES
0 50 100 150

D G J

MAP 55 /125

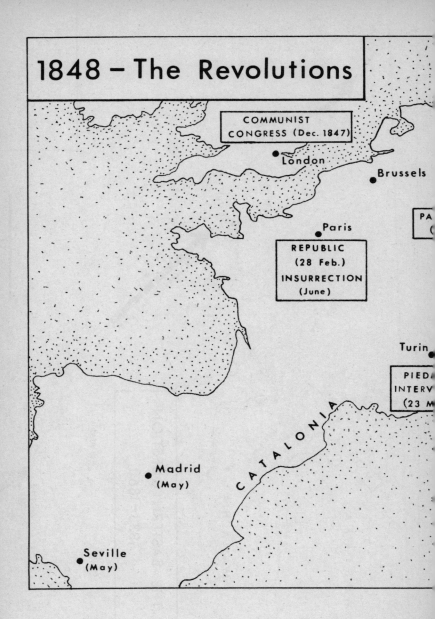

1848 – The Revolutions

COMMUNIST
CONGRESS (Dec. 1847)

● London

● Brussels

PA
(

● Paris

REPUBLIC
(28 Feb.)
INSURRECTION
(June)

Turin ●

PIED
INTERV
(23 M

CATALONIA

● Madrid
(May)

● Seville
(May)

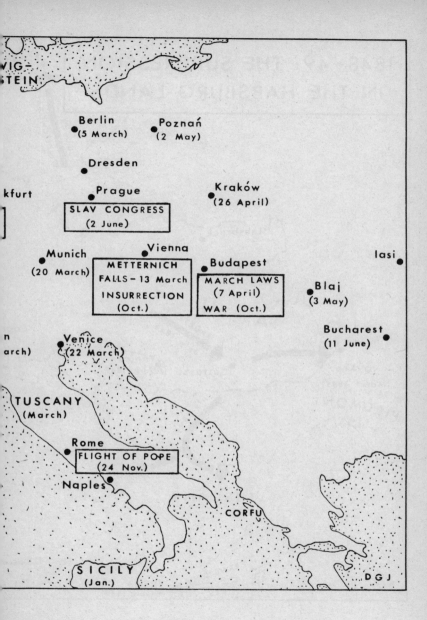

WIG-
STEIN

Berlin
(5 March)

Poznań
(2 May)

Dresden

kfurt

Prague

Kraków
(26 April)

SLAV CONGRESS
(2 June)

Munich
(20 March)

Vienna

Budapest

METTERNICH
FALLS – 13 March
INSURRECTION
(Oct.)

MARCH LAWS
(7 April)
WAR (Oct.)

Iasi

Blaj
(3 May)

Bucharest
(11 June)

n
arch)

Venice
(22 March)

TUSCANY
(March)

Rome
FLIGHT OF POPE
(24 Nov.)

Naples

CORFU

SICILY
(Jan.)

D G J

1848–49: THE SUPPRESSION IN THE HABSBURG LANDS

Prague

June 48
WINDISCHGRÄTZ

Vie

Danube Rr.

Innsbrück

AUSTRIA

RADETZKY
July 1848

Zagr

Milan

Venice
(Aug. 1849)

NOVARA
(March 1849)

Custozza

CRO

PIEDMONT

July 1849

TUSCANY

FRENCH
April 1849

Rome
(July 1849)

DGJ

0

M

Kraków

G A L I C I A

Kremsier

PASKEVICH
June 1849

Dec. 1848
WINDISCHGRÄTZ

HAYNAU–July 49

GÖRGEY
1849

Budapest

Debrecen

TRANSYLVANIA

H U N G A R Y

ČIČ – Oct. 1848

HAYNAU
Aug. 1849

Világos

Arad

PUCHNER
Oct. 48 –
Aug. 49

SERB
UPRISING
Oct.–Dec.
1848

BEM April
1849

Belgrade

Imperial Offensives

Hungarian Counter Offensives

French and Russian Interventions

Dates in parentheses refer to the
collapse of the revolution

200

e   s

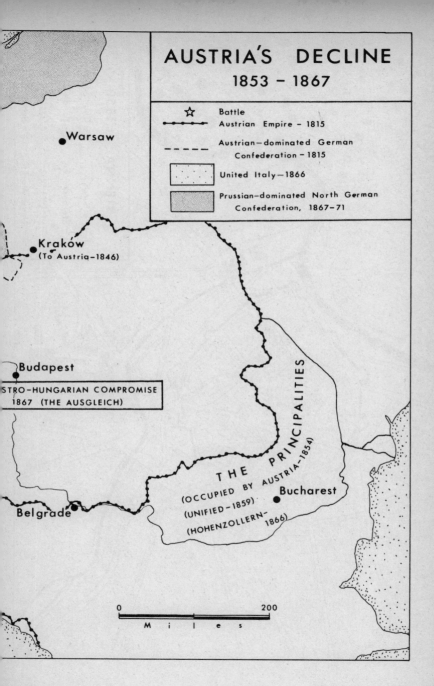

AUSTRIA'S DECLINE
1853 – 1867

☆ Battle
●━━━● Austrian Empire – 1815
- - - - - Austrian–dominated German
Confederation – 1815
United Italy – 1866
Prussian–dominated North German
Confederation, 1867–71

Warsaw

Kraków
(To Austria–1846)

Budapest

STRO-HUNGARIAN COMPROMISE
1867 (THE AUSGLEICH)

THE PRINCIPALITIES
(OCCUPIED BY AUSTRIA–1854)
(UNIFIED–1859)
(HOHENZOLLERN–1866)

Bucharest

Belgrade

0   200
M i l e s

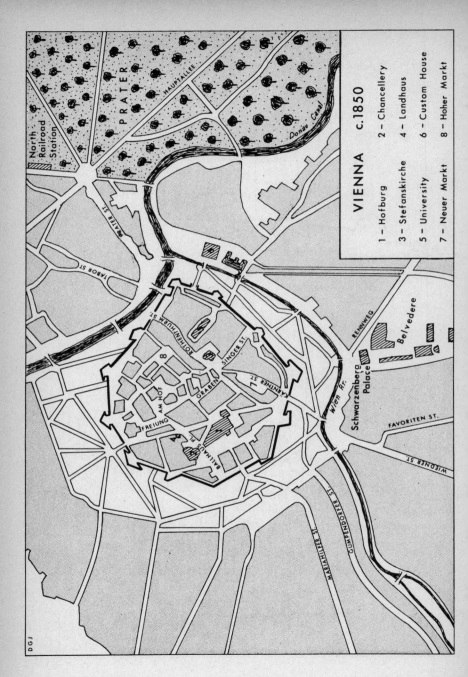

VIENNA c.1850

1 – Hofburg 2 – Chancellery
3 – Stefanskirche 4 – Landhaus
5 – University 6 – Custom House
7 – Neuer Markt 8 – Hoher Markt

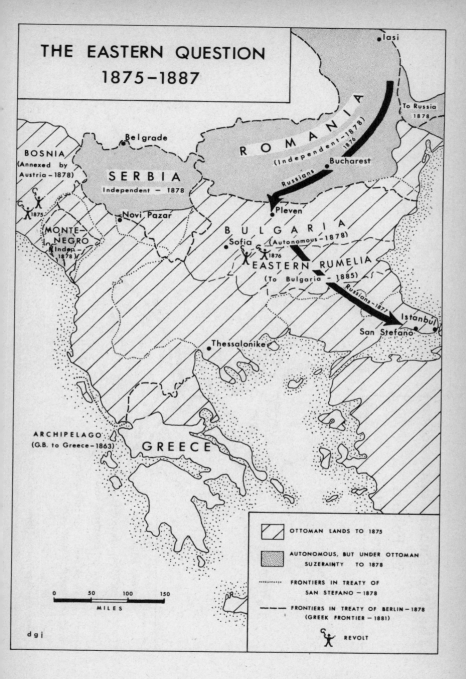

THE EASTERN QUESTION
1875-1887

Iasi

BOSNIA
(Annexed by
Austria - 1878)

Belgrade

To Russia
1878

ROMANIA
(Independent - 1878)
1876

SERBIA
Independent - 1878

Bucharest

Russians

MONTE-
NEGRO
(Indep -
1878)

Novi Pazar

Pleven

BULGARIA
(Autonomous - 1878)

Sofia
1876

EASTERN RUMELIA
(To Bulgaria - 1885)

Russians - 1877

Istanbul

San Stefano

Thessalonike

ARCHIPELAGO
(G.B. to Greece - 1863)

GREECE

OTTOMAN LANDS TO 1875

AUTONOMOUS, BUT UNDER OTTOMAN
SUZERAINTY TO 1878

FRONTIERS IN TREATY OF
SAN STEFANO - 1878

FRONTIERS IN TREATY OF BERLIN - 1878
(GREEK FRONTIER - 1881)

REVOLT

0   50   100   150
MILES

dgi

MAP 60   /133

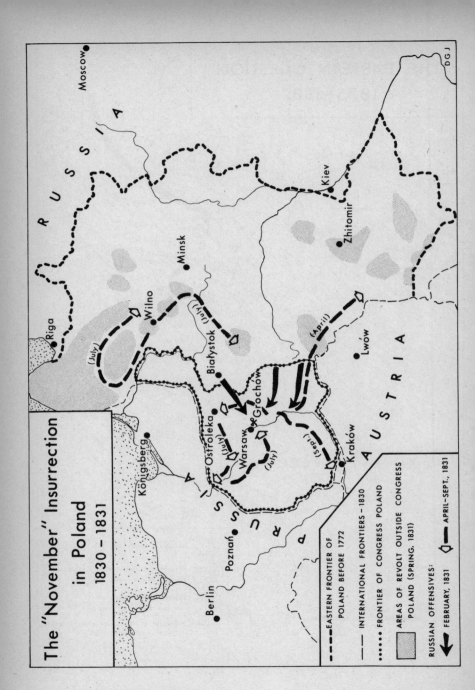

The "November" Insurrection
in Poland
1830 – 1831

Moscow

RUSSIA

Kiev

Zhitomir

Minsk

Riga

Wilno (July)

Białystok (July)

(April)

Lwów

Ostrołeka (July)

Grochów

Warsaw (July)

Königsberg

Kraków (Sept)

AUSTRIA

PRUSSIA

Poznań

Berlin

DGJ

EASTERN FRONTIER OF POLAND BEFORE 1772

INTERNATIONAL FRONTIERS – 1830

FRONTIER OF CONGRESS POLAND

AREAS OF REVOLT OUTSIDE CONGRESS POLAND (SPRING, 1831)

RUSSIAN OFFENSIVES:

FEBRUARY, 1831

APRIL–SEPT., 1831

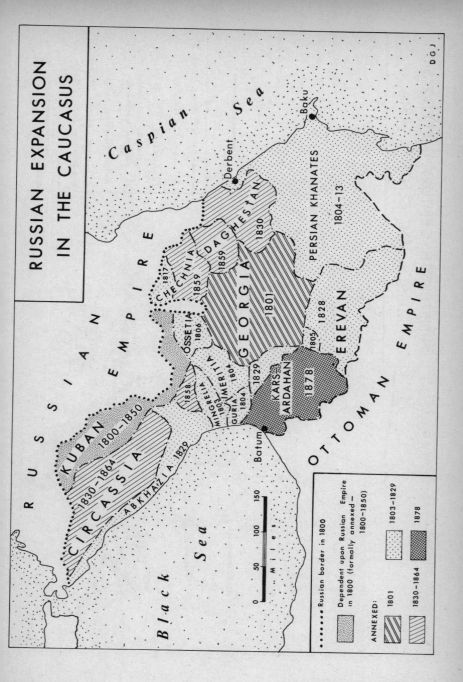

RUSSIAN EXPANSION IN THE CAUCASUS

Caspian Sea

Baku

Derbent

RUSSIAN EMPIRE

CHECHNIA 1817

DAGHESTAN 1859

1859

1830

GEORGIA 1801

PERSIAN KHANATES 1804-13

OSSETIA 1806

1828

1805

EREVAN

MINGRELIA 1803

1858

MERITIA 1804

1829

KARS ARDAHAN

1878

GURIA 1804

KUBAN 1800-1850

1830-1864

CIRCASSIA

ABKHAZIA 1829

Batum

OTTOMAN EMPIRE

Black Sea

MAP 62   /135

······ Russian border in 1800

Dependent upon Russian Empire in 1800 (formally annexed—1800-1850)

1803-1829

ANNEXED:

1801

1878

1830-1864

Miles

0   50   100   150

D G J

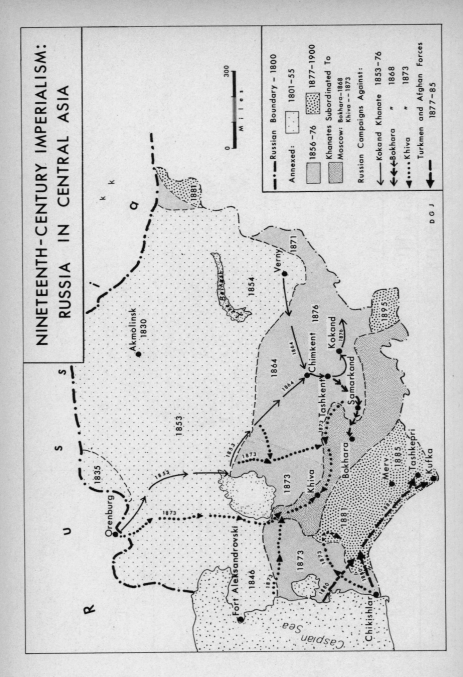

NINETEENTH-CENTURY IMPERIALISM: RUSSIA IN CENTRAL ASIA

Russian Boundary – 1800

Annexed:
1856–76
1877–1900

Khanates Subordinated To
Moscow: Bokhara–1868
Khiva – 1873

Russian Campaigns Against:
Kokand Khanate 1853–76
Bokhara   "   1868
Khiva   "   1873
Turkmen and Afghan Forces
1877–85

D G J

R   u   s   s   i

Akmolinsk
1830

1835

1853

1853

Orenburg

1873

Fort Aleksandrovski
1846

1873

Caspian Sea

Chikishlar

1880

1873

1873

Khiva

1873

Bokhara

188

Merv
1885

Tashkepri

Kufka

1877–85

Samarkand

Tashkent
1872

1864

Chimkent
1876

Kokand
1876

1864

1864

1853

1873

1854

Balkhash

Verny
1871

k   k
a   n

1881

1895

0   Miles   300

136/   MAP 63

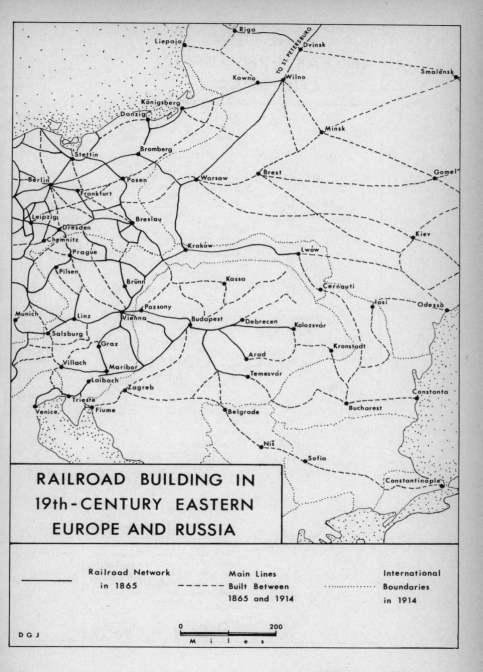

RAILROAD BUILDING IN
19th-CENTURY EASTERN
EUROPE AND RUSSIA

——————— Railroad Network
in 1865

– – – – – Main Lines
Built Between
1865 and 1914

············· International
Boundaries
in 1914

DGJ

0   200
M i l e s

THE JEWS IN EASTERN EUROPE AND RUSSIA

COURLAN

LITHUANIA

P R U S S I A

Berlin

1849 – 1.7 % JEWISH
1910 – 4.4 % "

Poznań

ACQUIRED BY PRUSSIA
1793 – 1815. JEWISH
DISABILITIES PARTLY
LIFTED IN 1812, FINALLY
IN 1867

Białystok

Warsaw

1900 – 37 % JEWISH

KINGDOM

OF POLAND

ACQ
JEWI
UKRA
AFTE
REDE
CONS

Prague

Kraków

Auschwitz

GALICIA

Lwów

ACQUIRED BY HABSBURGS IN
1772. JEWS BEGAN TO
ENTER OTHER HABSBURG
LANDS AFTER 1783.

A U S T R I A

Vienna

JEWS LARGELY EXCLUDED UNTIL
EMANCIPATION ACTS – 1848, 1867.

1857 – 1.3% JEWISH
1910 – 8.6%   "

Budapest

1850 – 11.3% JEWISH
1900 – 23.6 % "

Munkács

BUKOVINA

H U N G A R Y

Temesvár

THE SPANISH-SPEAKING SEPHARDIC JEWS
WERE DRIVEN OUT OF HUNGARY WITH
THE TURKS IN THE 17th CENTURY BUT
REMAINED IMPORTANT IN WALLACHIA
AND IN THE SOUTH SLAV LANDS UNTIL
WORLD WAR II.

WALLACHIA

O T T O M A N   E M P I R E

R U S S I A

● Moscow

LITHUANIAN
USSIAN URBAN
N JEWISH

ITE
nsk

● Smolensk

SOME CATEGORIES OF RICH
AND EDUCATED JEWS ALLOWED
TO SETTLE OUTSIDE PALE
AFTER 1859

SIA

● Gomel

IN 1772–1815.
TO NEW RUSSIA,
SUS ALLOWED
SE AREAS,
D 1887,
E OF JEWISH

● Kiev

K R A I N E

1897–30% OF UKRAINIAN
URBAN POPULATION
JEWISH

RABIA

● Kishinev

● Odessa

MAJOR SOURCES OF JEWISH
EMIGRATION DURING 19th CENTURY

――――― INTERNATIONAL FRONTIERS, 1815

- - - - - INTERNAL FRONTIERS

⟵ JEWISH MIGRATIONS

●—●—● THE PALE OF JEWISH SETTLEMENT

0   200

M i l e s

● Poltava   ● Kharkov

● Ekaterinoslav

● Nikolaev   T A U R I D A   ● Taganrog

CAUCASUS

EMIGRATION
TO U.S.A.

● Sevastopol   ● Ialta

Black   Sea   D G J

Part V
The Twentieth Century

In the twentieth century, new catastrophes afflicted Russia and Eastern Europe. These lands remained in many ways culturally subordinate to the West, but increasingly, in political matters, they achieved autonomy from Western Europe and came to play independent roles in world affairs.

Before and After World War I (MAPS 66–93)

It was no accident that the immediate cause of World War I was a political assassination in 1914 in Bosnia. For a decade before 1914, the peoples of the Balkans had been challenging the presumption that their destinies were dependent upon the will of the great European powers. By 1908, the spirit of independence was so strong in the Balkans that when Britain and Russia announced that they would seek a settlement for the Macedonian question, they provoked the nationalist and democratic "Young Turk" Revolution in Constantinople. When Austria seized this occasion to annex Bosnia-Herzegovina and to encourage Bulgaria to declare its independence of the Turks, Serbia became so belligerent that all Europe was brought to the brink of war.

In 1911, Italy's invasion of Turkish-dominated Libya served as a pretext for Serbia, Bulgaria, Montenegro, and Greece to band together. In the autumn of 1912, they declared war on Turkey and, without the aid of any of the great powers, put an end to the centuries-old Ottoman dominion in Europe. During the following year, to the further consternation of the great powers, a new combination of little Balkan states (Serbia, Greece, Romania, and Turkey) fought a successful war against Bulgaria (*Map 66*).

The end of nineteenth-century imperialistic power over the Balkans was fully evident before World War I. In the winter of 1913–14, Austria sought to counteract the gains of Serbia and Greece in the Second Balkan War by creating a new state, Albania. This intervention set the stage for the assassination of the Austrian Archduke Francis Ferdinand by South Slav nationalists at Sarajevo on June 28, 1914—the spark that set off the war (*Maps 77, 78*). Even with the war in full course, Bulgaria and Romania continued to work for their own national interests. Bulgaria forced the great warring alliances to compete for its favors, entering the war in October, 1915, after the Central Powers had offered it large parts of Serbia. Romania, committed by a 1914 treaty to fight on the German side, joined the Allies in mid-1916 in response to offers of Hungarian lands. Subsequently, Romania changed sides twice.

The 1905 Revolution in Russia marked a new high point in another kind of emancipation struggle. In 1904, Tsar Nicholas II (1894–1917), following an expansionist policy in the Far East, engaged his country in a war with Japan (*Maps 67, 68*). The struggle overtaxed Russia's limited industrial and transportation capacities and led to humiliating defeat at the hands of non-Europeans and to internal chaos that aggravated the serious discontent already existing at almost all levels of the social order (*Maps 70–74*). In October, 1905, against a background of massive industrial strikes, turmoil among the national minorities, and widespread peasant unrest, liberal and socialist political agitators forced the Tsar to accept the limitations of a constitution. In the months that followed, however, the Tsar suppressed the revolutionary elements by military means and reneged on some of his political concessions. Nonetheless, 1905 showed that in the twentieth century, the Russians, like the Balkan peoples, were ready to take up arms for the right to govern themselves.

World War I and the peace settlements that followed it effected great changes in Eastern Europe (*Maps 82–88*). The war destroyed Austria-Hungary and the Russo-Prussian control system in Poland. Finland, Estonia, Latvia, Lithuania, and Poland achieved national statehood. Bohemia combined with the Slovak lands of northern Hungary to form Czechoslovakia. Serbia combined with Croatia, Slovenia, Bosnia, and Montenegro to form Yugoslavia. Hungary escaped from its league with Austria to become an independent nation, and Romania acquired Transylvania and Bessarabia.

In Russia, the war precipitated a new showdown between the people and the government. Civil disturbances and soldiers' mutinies at St. Petersburg during the second week of March, 1917, brought down the autocracy, forcing the Tsar to abdicate. The "March Revolution" was followed by the virtual collapse of Russia's economy and its ability to resist German aggression. In this situation, it was not possible to establish a new political regime that could restore order, and the Empire simply fell apart until November, 1917, when the extremist Bolshevik faction of the Russian Social Democratic Party seized power. The Bolsheviks, led by V. I. Lenin (1917–24), promptly set about building a Communist social order in Russia and, in order to gain time, sought to get out of the war. They signed the concessionary Brest-Litovsk Treaty with the Germans (March, 1918), surrendering Poland, the Baltic area, Bessarabia, the Ukraine, and—in the Transcaucasian region—Kars, Ardahan, and Batumi (*Map 79*).

But the Bolsheviks were not destined to obtain peace in 1918. Instead, a civil war raged until 1921 between Bolshevik ("Red") and anti-Bolshevik ("White") forces (*Maps 80, 81*). This fighting was complicated by the actions of important national groups living within the crumbling Empire (Belorussians, Ukrainians, Armenians, Georgians, Azerbaijanians, and the Moslem peoples of Central Asia, who tried, with varying degrees of success, to win autonomy or national independence (*Map 82*). The civil strife was further complicated by the intervention of Allied forces from Japan, Great Britain, the United States, and France, as well as by war with Poland (*Maps 80, 81, 86*). When peace finally came, the old Empire was reorganized as the Union of Soviet Socialist Republics (1923), each major nationality receiving its own political organization within the Union (*Map 82*). The Russian people had paid a terrible price in blood for their revolution and had obtained for their pains something very similar to the old autocracy.

In Eastern Europe, peace brought much more than simple territorial independence. Without exception, the new states were constitutional; several made sincere efforts to achieve social democratization; and most of them joined the League of Nations. In effect, the Versailles settlement represented a political culmination of nineteenth-century liberalism. Moreover, in the "New Europe," the West was no longer politically supreme, for the victorious Allies deliberately assigned the little eastern states major roles in the balance of European power.

Unfortunately, the "New Eastern Europe" was built on unsteady foundations. Foremost among these was economic weakness (*Map 76*). Even before the war, almost all the eastern lands had suffered from having overwhelmingly rural economies in an increasingly industrial age. After the war, this defect was exacerbated by rapid population increases, the closing of former channels of emigration, and the formal acceptance by Poland, Hungary, Bulgaria, and Greece of sizable displaced populations. Furthermore, Moldavia, Serbia, and much of Poland had been devastated by the war; and the defeated nations—Bulgaria, Hungary, Austria, Turkey, and Germany—had to raise large sums for indemnity payments. Finally, no sooner had postwar reconstruction efforts begun to show results, than the world wheat market collapsed (1928–29) and the world financial depression followed (1929–31).

A second weakness of postwar Eastern Europe stemmed from the fact that it was easier to dream and talk of new national states than to create them. In the case of Poland, for example, the territory of the old Polish-Lithuanian Union, destroyed between 1772 and 1795, was considerably larger than Polish territory in 1918 (*Map 86*). Even ethnic territories were indefinable, for in varying degrees in the Poznań-Danzig area, Silesia, and the eastern frontier zone, Poles were interspersed with Germans, Czechs, Ukrainians, Belorussians, and Lithuanians. Similarly, Czechoslovakia, Greater Romania, and Yugoslavia possessed no clear ethnic frontiers, particularly where their new boundaries lay within what had formerly been Hungary (*Maps 83, 84, 85*). Solutions to the frontier problems of Poland and Pannonia were finally made by means of Romanian and Czech invasions of Hungary, a Polish war with Russia, and Allied dictation (*Maps 83, 86*).

Other trouble spots lay in the Balkans, where Greeks, Slavs, and Turks had lived together—albeit in mutual hatred—for centuries (*Maps 85, 87*). A temporary solution had been found for the Macedonian problem during the Balkan Wars of 1912–13: Most of the area went to Serbia (*Map 66*). In Thrace, a solution was suggested by the fact that Bulgaria had fought on the losing side in World War I: Most of Thrace, therefore, was assigned to Greece. The problem of what to do with Turkey presented major difficulties at the end of the war. In 1915 and 1917, the British and the French had promised Turkish ethnic territories to Russia and Italy in return for their participation in the war. The Greeks, too, considered that they had a just claim to part of western Anatolia. At the end of the war, the Bolshevik government in Moscow renounced all "imperialistic acquisitions"; but the Italians sought to hold the Allies to their promises, and the Greeks dreamed of re-establishing the Byzantine Empire. It took a new revolution in Turkey, a Greco-Turkish war, and drastic population exchanges to settle the matter.

In sum, postwar Eastern Europe was founded on the arbitrary resolution of a great number of national territorial problems that left every country of the area burdened with sizeable minority groups and with strong resentments against its neighbors.

A third major weakness in the foundations of postwar Eastern Europe was the territorial revisionism, potential and actual, of the states that had formerly dominated the area. Only two proved willing to reconcile themselves to the peace settlements. Austria did so because it had nearly been abolished. For Turkey, the initial postwar solution was so drastic that Turkish nationalists under Kemal Ataturk (1921–38) took up arms, obtained a revision of the peace treaty in 1923, and, thereafter, supported the status quo.

Russia lost more territory through the peace settlements of 1917–21 than did any other European power, but until the very end of the interwar period, Russia abstained from open revisionism. Lenin and his successor, Stalin (1924–53), needed to maintain peace in order to effect the nation's economic recovery (*Map 89*). After 1928, Stalin had an even greater need for peace in order to drive Russia through the forced industrialization that is often called the "Second Bolshevik Revolution." Therefore, the fires of revisionism were banked, but the losses were not forgotten. Few believed that the Soviet behemoth, with its burgeoning industrial might and its talk of world Communist revolution, would not some day seek to collect for the damages suffered when it was too weak to defend itself.

If circumstances in Austria, Turkey, and Russia brought reluctant acceptance of the new Eastern Europe, in Hungary, Italy, and Germany, a revisionist spirit prevailed (*Map 88*). In Hungary, this was because the nation had been brutally dismembered; but the country was now so small that it could do nothing on its own. Italy and Germany, however, had achieved statehood only in the latter part of the nineteenth century and had fought World War I in the expectation that they would complete their national unification and acquire greater national dignity by absorbing Eastern European lands. Disappointed in 1918 and after, they complained bitterly. Outwardly, the Italians had little real justification for complaint. Fighting the war on the winning side, they had managed to incorporate all Italian ethnic lands (*Map 85*). But severe internal political tensions in the country were aggravated when the United States, Great Britain, and France denied Italy promised territories in Dalmatia. When the Fascists, under Mussolini, seized power (1922), they made revisionism a permanent feature of Italian interwar foreign policy.

The Germans had far more reason for discontent than the Italians. They had lost the war. Lands previously inside the Reich were now assigned to Poland (*Map 86*), and others, formerly within German-dominated Austria, had gone to Czechoslovakia (*Map 84*). In addition, the war had stripped Germany of its overseas colonies, causing a catastrophic financial collapse. When the world depression brought about a second economic debacle, the stage was set for the accession to power in 1933 of Adolf Hitler and his violently nationalistic National Socialist German Workers' Party. Within six months after taking office, Hitler withdrew Germany from the League of Nations, symbolizing his challenge to the status quo.

Because of their many weaknesses, the new states of Eastern Europe collapsed rapidly when they were challenged by Hitler (*Maps 90–92*). In March, 1938, only five years after coming to power, he demanded and obtained the annexation of Austria to Germany (*Anschluss*). He then bluffed the major western nations into a partial dismemberment of Czechoslovakia (Munich, September, 1938) and encouraged the Hungarians to seize ethnic Magyar lands in Slovakia (*Maps 84, 90*). In March, 1939, he completed the dissolution of Czechoslovakia by annexing all the Czech lands to the German Reich and by establishing a puppet Slovak state in what remained. In April, 1939, his ally Mussolini annexed Albania.

Hitler next turned to his territorial ambitions in Poland (*Map 90*). In August, 1939, he secured an alliance with the Soviet Union; Stalin had, at last, become convinced that he could gain more from a pact with Germany than from cooperation with Britain, France, and Poland. In September, Hitler precipitated World War II by invading Poland and conquering the land before the end of the month. During the spring of 1940, he overran Western Europe (*Map 92*); thereafter, in conjunction with the Soviet Union and Hungary, he turned to the partitioning of Romania.

Meanwhile, the Russians made their challenge to the status quo in Eastern Europe by sharing in the new partition of Poland and embarking upon a war with Finland (*Map 90*). Unable to achieve a decisive victory in the "Winter War," they forced the Finns to sign a peace treaty (March, 1940) ceding Finnish lands north of Leningrad to the Soviet Union. They then turned their attention to Eastern Europe, where Hitler's successes increasingly menaced Soviet interests. In the summer of 1940, they annexed the small Baltic states, Estonia, Latvia, and Lithuania, and demanded that Hitler recognize the Soviet sphere of influence in the Balkans. Hitler, unable to win the Battle of Britain and angered by Soviet pressures in the East, resolved that the Soviet Union must be destroyed.

Before Hitler could move against the Russians, however, Mussolini attacked Greece (October, 1940) and became embroiled in military difficulties there (*Map 91*). Therefore, in the spring of 1941, Hitler delayed his invasion of the Soviet Union in order to settle the Balkan question. His armies overran Yugoslavia in two weeks. He created a new fascistic Croatian state and a Greater Bulgaria and then proceeded to drive the Allied forces out of Greece. On June 22, 1941, when the German invasion of Russia finally began (*Map 93*), not one of the states of Eastern Europe remained as it had been established after World War I (*Map 92*). For Eastern Europe, the first era of autonomy in the twentieth century was over.

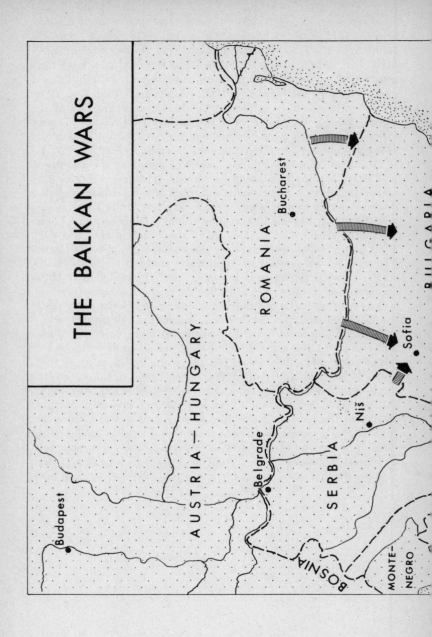

THE BALKAN WARS

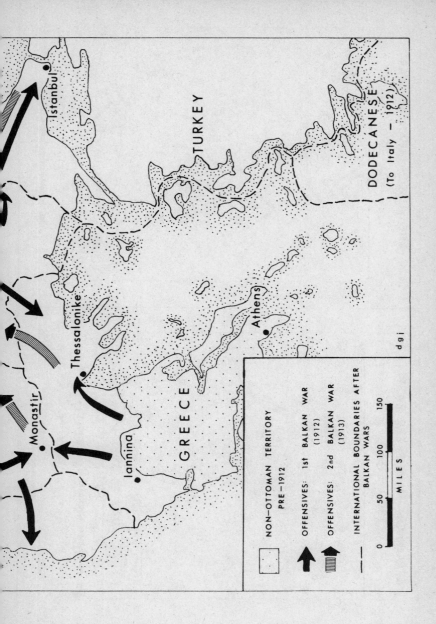

TURKEY

DODECANESE
(To Italy — 1912)

Istanbul

Thessaloníke

Athens

Monastir

Iannina

GREECE

dgi

NON-OTTOMAN TERRITORY
PRE–1912

OFFENSIVES: 1st BALKAN WAR
(1912)

OFFENSIVES: 2nd BALKAN WAR
(1913)

INTERNATIONAL BOUNDARIES AFTER
BALKAN WARS

0   50   100   150

MILES

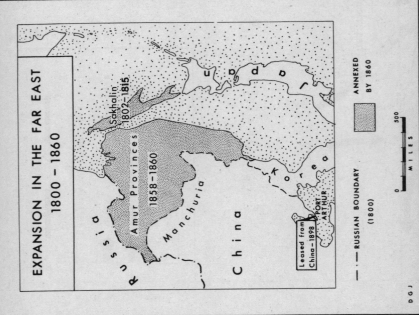

THE RUSSO–JAPANESE WAR
1904–1905

POSITION OF FORCES AT END OF WAR

JAPANESE NAVAL ATTACKS (2/8–9/1904)

RUSSIA

Vladivostok

CHINA

Port Arthur

Seoul

KOREA

RUSSIANS

JAPANESE

RUSSIAN FLEET

Tsushima Strait

Pusan

JAPANESE FLEET (5/27/1905)

JAPAN

0   300
MILES

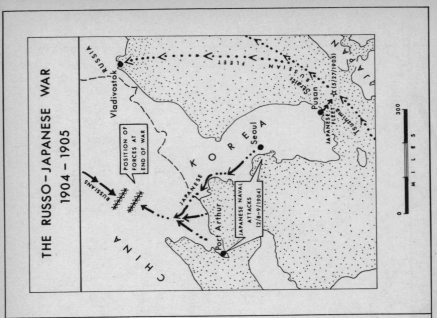

EXPANSION IN THE FAR EAST
1800 – 1860

Russia

Sakhalin 1802–1815

Amur Provinces 1858–1860

Manchuria

China

Korea

Amur

PORT ARTHUR
Leased from China–1898

— · — · — RUSSIAN BOUNDARY (1800)

ANNEXED BY 1860

0   500
MILES

D G J

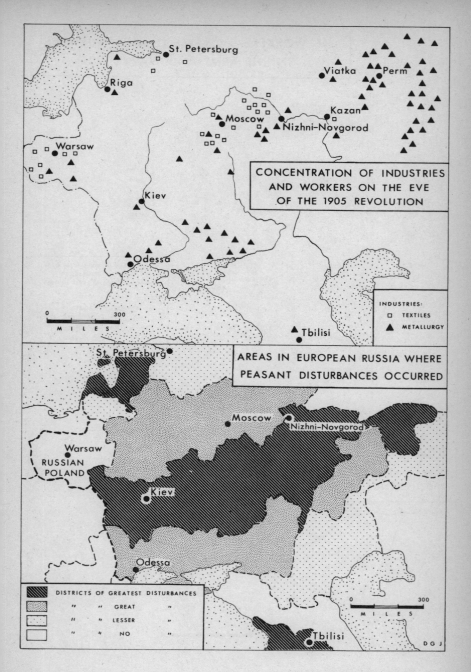

CONCENTRATION OF INDUSTRIES
AND WORKERS ON THE EVE
OF THE 1905 REVOLUTION

St. Petersburg

Riga

Viatka Perm

Moscow

Kazan

Nizhni-Novgorod

Warsaw

Kiev

Odessa

INDUSTRIES:

☐ TEXTILES

▲ METALLURGY

0   300
M I L E S

Tbilisi

AREAS IN EUROPEAN RUSSIA WHERE
PEASANT DISTURBANCES OCCURRED

St. Petersburg

Moscow   Nizhni-Novgorod

Warsaw
RUSSIAN
POLAND

Kiev

Odessa

DISTRICTS OF GREATEST DISTURBANCES
    "   " GREAT   "
    "   " LESSER   "
    "   " NO   "

0   300
M I L E S

Tbilisi

D G J

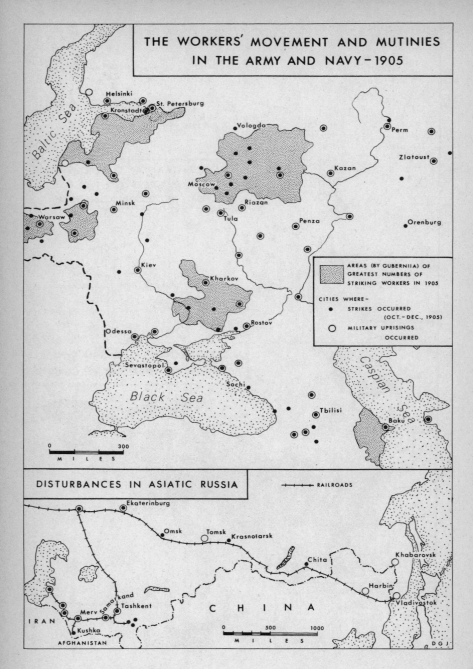

THE WORKERS' MOVEMENT AND MUTINIES
IN THE ARMY AND NAVY – 1905

Helsinki
St. Petersburg
Kronstadt
Vologda
Perm
Zlatoust
Baltic Sea
Kazan
Minsk
Moscow
Warsaw
Riazan
Orenburg
Tula
Penza
Kiev
Kharkov
Caspian Sea
Odessa
Rostov
Sevastopol
Sochi
Black Sea
Tbilisi
Baku

AREAS (BY GUBERNIIA) OF
GREATEST NUMBERS OF
STRIKING WORKERS IN 1905
CITIES WHERE –
● STRIKES OCCURRED
(OCT. – DEC., 1905)
○ MILITARY UPRISINGS
OCCURRED

0 ⎯ 300
M I L E S

DISTURBANCES IN ASIATIC RUSSIA

+—+—+ RAILROADS

Ekaterinburg
Omsk
Tomsk
Krasnotarsk
Chita
Khabarovsk
Samarkand
Merv
Tashkent
Harbin
IRAN
Kushka
Vladivostok
AFGHANISTAN
C H I N A

0 ⎯ 500 ⎯ 1000
M I L E S

D G J

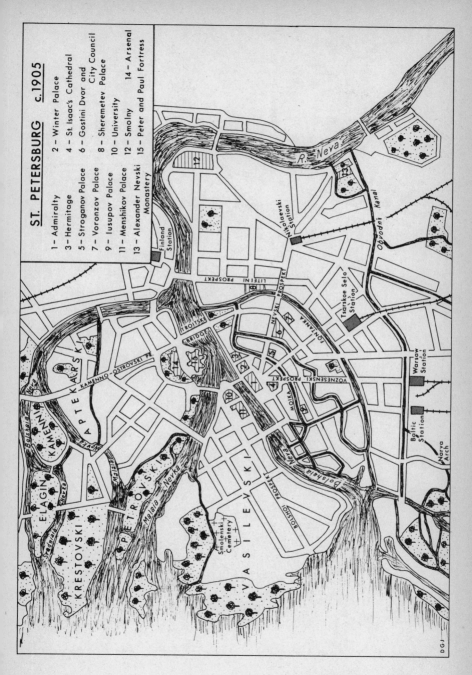

ST. PETERSBURG c.1905

1 – Admiralty
2 – Winter Palace
3 – Hermitage
4 – St. Isaac's Cathedral
5 – Stroganov Palace
6 – Gostini Dvor and City Council
7 – Voronzov Palace
8 – Sheremetev Palace
9 – Iusupov Palace
10 – University
11 – Menshikov Palace
12 – Smolny
13 – Alexander Nevski Monastery
14 – Arsenal
15 – Peter and Paul Fortress

R. Neva

Obvodni Kanal

Nikolaevski Station

Finland Station

LITEINI PROSPEKT

Tsarskoe Selo Station

FONTANKA

Warsaw Station

TROITSK BRIDGE

KAMENNO-OSTROVSKI PR.

VOZNESENSKI PROSPEKT

MOIKA

Baltic Station

Narva Arch

APTEKARSKI

ELAGIN

KAMENNI

Bolshaia Neva

Srednaia

Malaia Nevka

KRESTOVSKI

PETROVSKI

Malaia Nevka

Malaia Neva

Smolenski Cemetery

V A S I L E V S K I

BOLSHOI PROSPEKT

Bolshaia Neva

D·G·J

MAP 73   /153

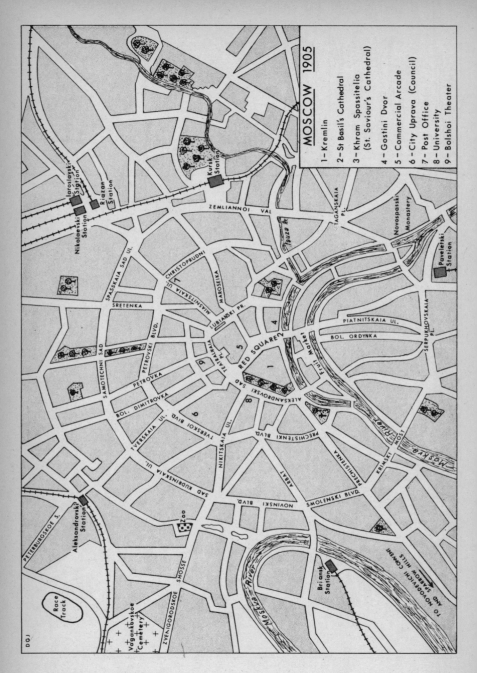

MOSCOW 1905

1 – Kremlin
2 – St Basil's Cathedral
3 – Khram Spassitelia
    (St. Saviour's Cathedral)
4 – Gostini Dvor
5 – Commercial Arcade
6 – City Uprava (Council)
7 – Post Office
8 – University
9 – Bolshoi Theater

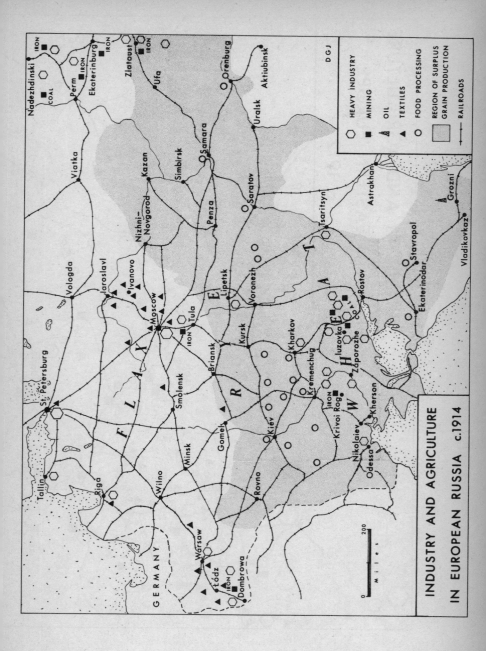

INDUSTRY AND AGRICULTURE
IN EUROPEAN RUSSIA c.1914

HEAVY INDUSTRY ⬡
MINING ■
OIL ▲
TEXTILES ▲
FOOD PROCESSING ○
REGION OF SURPLUS GRAIN PRODUCTION
RAILROADS

MAP 75   / 155

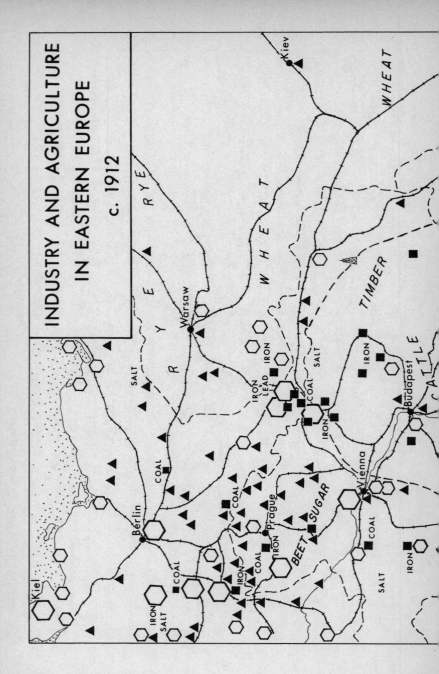

INDUSTRY AND AGRICULTURE IN EASTERN EUROPE c. 1912

Kiel

Berlin

Warsaw

Kiev

Prague

Vienna

Budapest

RYE

RYE

WHEAT

WHEAT

WHEAT

TIMBER

CATTLE

SALT

COAL

COAL

COAL

COAL

COAL

COAL

COAL

IRON

IRON

IRON

IRON

IRON

IRON

IRON

LEAD

SALT

SALT

SALT

BEET SUGAR

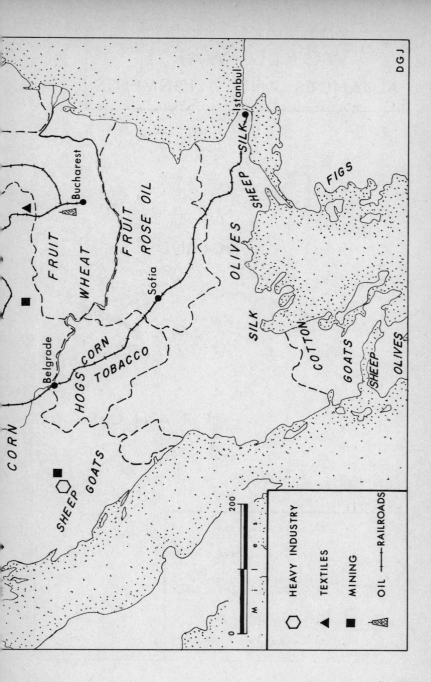

157

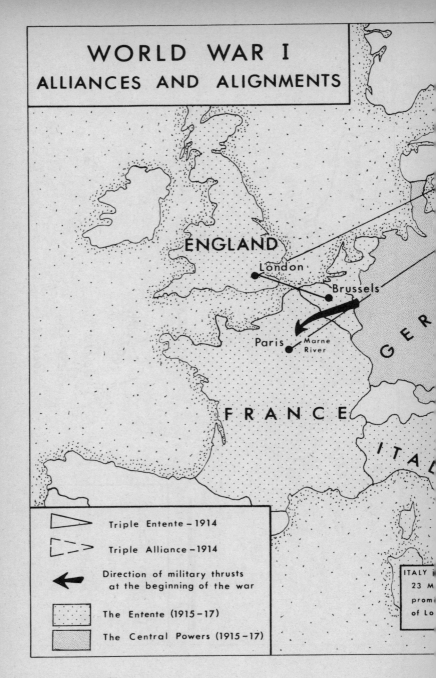

WORLD WAR I
ALLIANCES AND ALIGNMENTS

ENGLAND

London

Brussels

Paris · Marne River

FRANCE

GER

ITAL

Triple Entente – 1914

Triple Alliance – 1914

Direction of military thrusts at the beginning of the war

The Entente (1915–17)

The Central Powers (1915–17)

ITALY
23 M
prom
of Lo

ROMANIA joined the Allies 18 August 1916, made peace on 7 May 1918, but rejoined the Allies on the eve of the victory.

BULGARIA joined the Central Powers after the Gallipoli Campaign bogged down 14 Oct. 1915.

THE ALLIES crossed Greek waters to reach Gallipoli in March 1915, anded at Salonika in Nov. 1915 and forced Greece to declare war in June 1917.

DGJ

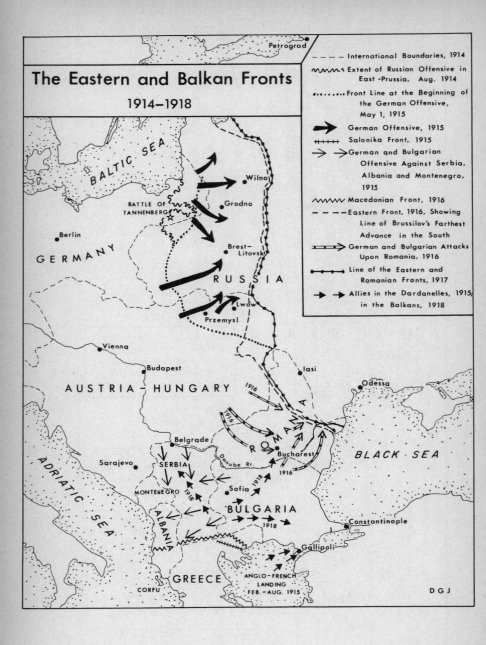

The Eastern and Balkan Fronts

1914–1918

Legend:

- — — — International Boundaries, 1914
- Extent of Russian Offensive in East-Prussia, Aug. 1914
- .... Front Line at the Beginning of the German Offensive, May 1, 1915
- German Offensive, 1915
- +++++ Salonika Front, 1915
- German and Bulgarian Offensive Against Serbia, Albania and Montenegro, 1915
- Macedonian Front, 1916
- — — — Eastern Front, 1916, Showing Line of Brussilov's Farthest Advance in the South
- German and Bulgarian Attacks Upon Romania, 1916
- Line of the Eastern and Romanian Fronts, 1917
- Allies in the Dardanelles, 1915; in the Balkans, 1918

Petrograd

BALTIC SEA

Wilno

BATTLE OF TANNENBERG

Grodno

Berlin

Brest-Litovski

GERMANY

RUSSIA

Lwow

Przemysl

Vienna

Budapest

Iasi

AUSTRIA - HUNGARY

1916

Odessa

1916

ROMANIA

Belgrade

Danube Rr.

Bucharest

BLACK SEA

Sarajevo

SERBIA

1916

MONTENEGRO 1918

Sofia 1918

ADRIATIC SEA

ALBANIA

BULGARIA

1918

Constantinople

Gallipoli

GREECE

ANGLO-FRENCH LANDING FEB.- AUG. 1915

CORFU

DGJ

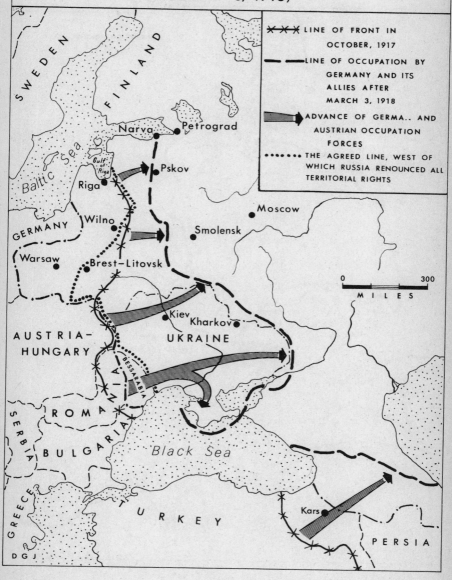

THE BREST-LITOVSK SETTLEMENT
(March 3, 1918)

LINE OF FRONT IN OCTOBER, 1917

LINE OF OCCUPATION BY GERMANY AND ITS ALLIES AFTER MARCH 3, 1918

ADVANCE OF GERMA.. AND AUSTRIAN OCCUPATION FORCES

THE AGREED LINE, WEST OF WHICH RUSSIA RENOUNCED ALL TERRITORIAL RIGHTS

SWEDEN

FINLAND

Baltic Sea

Gulf of Riga

Narva

Petrograd

Pskov

Riga

GERMANY

Wilno

Moscow

Smolensk

Warsaw

Brest–Litovsk

0   300

MILES

AUSTRIA-HUNGARY

Kiev

Kharkov

UKRAINE

BESSARABIA

ROMANIA

SERBIA

BULGARIA

Black Sea

GREECE

TURKEY

Kars

PERSIA

D G J

MAP 79   /161

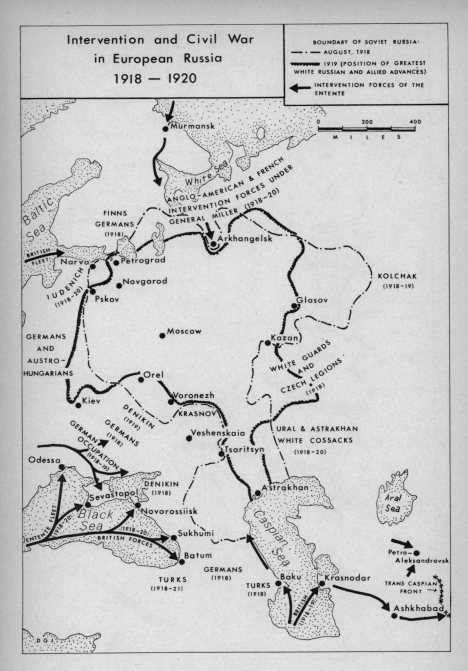

Intervention and Civil War
in European Russia
1918 — 1920

BOUNDARY OF SOVIET RUSSIA:
— · — AUGUST, 1918
••••••••• 1919 (POSITION OF GREATEST
WHITE RUSSIAN AND ALLIED ADVANCES)
← INTERVENTION FORCES OF THE
ENTENTE

0   200   400
M I L E S

Baltic Sea

White Sea

Murmansk

FINNS
GERMANS
(1918)

ANGLO-AMERICAN & FRENCH
INTERVENTION FORCES UNDER
GENERAL MILLER (1918-20)

Arkhangelsk

KOLCHAK
(1918-19)

BRITISH
FLEET

Narva

Petrograd

IUDENICH
(1918-20)

Pskov

Novgorod

Glasov

Kazan

Moscow

GERMANS
AND
AUSTRO-
HUNGARIANS

WHITE GUARDS
AND
CZECH LEGIONS
(1918)

Orel

Kiev

DENIKIN
(1919)

Voronezh

KRASNOV

GERMANS
(1918)

GERMAN
OCCUPATION
(1918-19)

Veshenskaia

URAL & ASTRAKHAN
WHITE COSSACKS
(1918-20)

Tsaritsyn

Odessa

DENIKIN
(1918)

Sevastopol

Black
Sea

Novorossiisk

Astrakhan

Aral
Sea

ENTENTE FLEET (1918-20)

(1918-20)

BRITISH FORCES

Sukhumi

Caspian Sea

Petro-
Aleksandrovsk

Batum

GERMANS
(1918)

TURKS
(1918-21)

TURKS
(1918)

Baku

BRITISH
1918-19

Krasnodar

TRANS CASPIAN
FRONT

Ashkhabad

D G J.

162 /   MAP 80

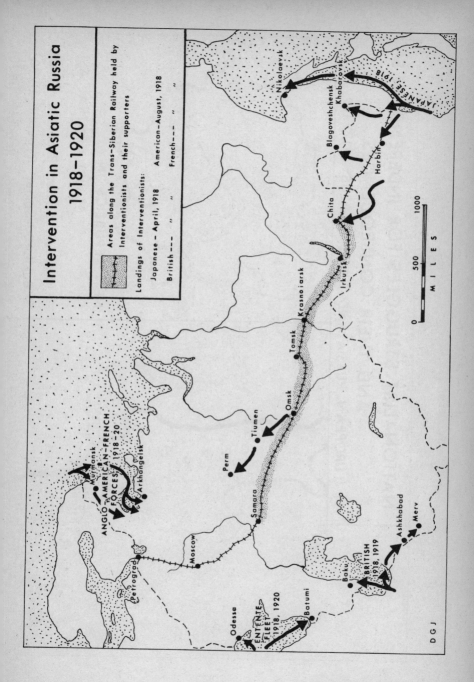

Intervention in Asiatic Russia 1918–1920

Areas along the Trans-Siberian Railway held by Interventionists and their supporters:

Landings of Interventionists:

Japanese – April, 1918   American–August, 1918

British – "   "   "   French – "   "   "

JAPANESE 1918

Nikolaevsk

Blagoveshchensk

Khabarovsk

Harbin

Chita

Irkutsk

Krasnoiarsk

Tomsk

Omsk

Tiumen

Perm

Samara

Moscow

Petrograd

Murmansk

ANGLO-AMERICAN-FRENCH
FORCES, 1918–20

Arkhangelsk

Baku

Ashkhabad

Merv

BRITISH
1918, 1919

Odessa

Batumi

ENTENTE
FLEET
1918, 1920

1000

500

M I L E S

0

D G J

MAP 81   /163

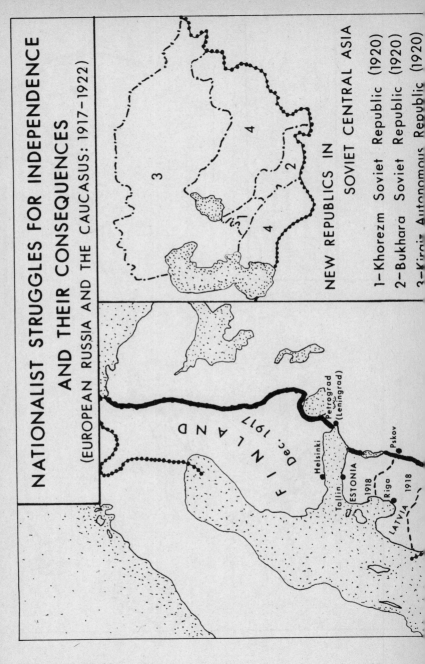

NATIONALIST STRUGGLES FOR INDEPENDENCE AND THEIR CONSEQUENCES
(EUROPEAN RUSSIA AND THE CAUCASUS: 1917–1922)

NEW REPUBLICS IN SOVIET CENTRAL ASIA

1—Khorezm Soviet Republic (1920)
2—Bukhara Soviet Republic (1920)
3—Kirgiz Autonomous Republic (1920)

FINLAND

Dec. 1917

Petrograd (Leningrad)

Helsinki

Tallin

ESTONIA 1918

Riga 1918

LATVIA

Pskov

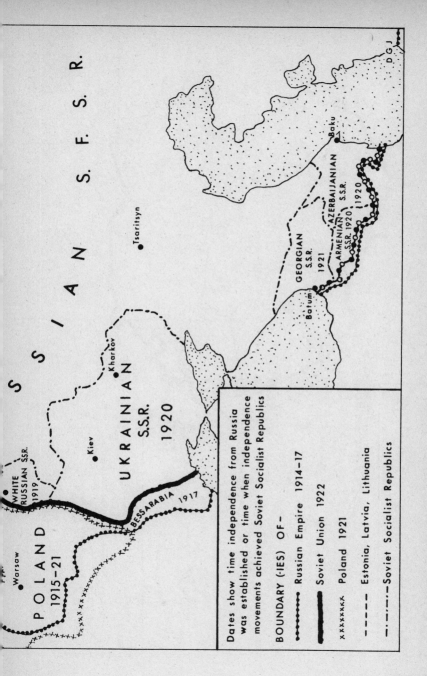

Dates show time independence from Russia was established or time when independence movements achieved Soviet Socialist Republics

BOUNDARY (-IES) OF—

●●●●●●● Russian Empire 1914–17

━━━━ Soviet Union 1922

xxxxxxx Poland 1921

────── Estonia, Latvia, Lithuania

─·─·─ Soviet Socialist Republics

RUSSIAN S. F. S. R.

Baku

Tsaritsyn

AZERBAIJANIAN S.S.R.
1920

ARMENIAN S.S.R. 1920

GEORGIAN S.S.R. 1921

Batum

Kharkov

UKRAINIAN S.S.R. 1920

Kiev

WHITE RUSSIAN SSR. 1919

BESSARABIA 1917

Warsaw

POLAND 1915–21

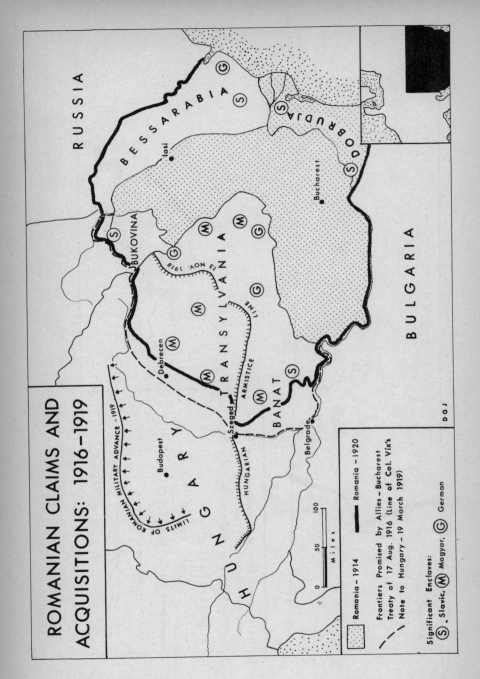

ROMANIAN CLAIMS AND ACQUISITIONS: 1916–1919

RUSSIA

BESSARABIA

Iasi

BUKOVINA

DOBRUDJA

Bucharest

TRANSYLVANIA

13 NOV. 1918 LINE

ARMISTICE LINE

Debrecen

BANAT

Szeged

HUNGARIAN

Budapest

HUNGARY

LIMITS OF ROMANIAN MILITARY ADVANCE – 1919

Belgrade

BULGARIA

D G J

Romania – 1914

Romania – 1920

Frontiers Promised by Allies – Bucharest Treaty of 17 Aug. 1916 (Line of Col. Vix's Note to Hungary – 19 March 1919)

Significant Enclaves:

Ⓢ – Slavic, Ⓜ Magyar, Ⓖ German

Miles
0   50   100

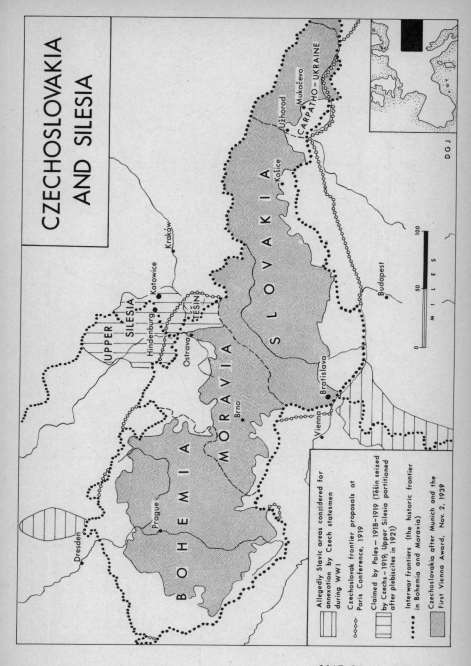

CZECHOSLOVAKIA AND SILESIA

BOHEMIA

MORAVIA

SLOVAKIA

UPPER SILESIA

SILESIA

TĚŠÍN

Dresden

Prague

Brno

Kraków

Katowice

Hindenburg

Ostrava

Bratislava

Vienna

Budapest

Košice

Užhorod

Mukačevo

CARPATHO–UKRAINE

Allegedly Slavic areas considered for
annexation by Czech statesmen
during WWI

Czechoslovak frontier proposals at
Paris Conference, 1919

Claimed by Poles – 1918–1919 (Těšín seized
by Czechs – 1919, Upper Silesia partitioned
after plebiscites in 1921)

Interwar frontiers (the historic frontier
in Bohemia and Moravia)

Czechoslovakia after Munich and the
First Vienna Award, Nov. 2, 1939

MILES

0   50   100

D G J

MAP 84   /167

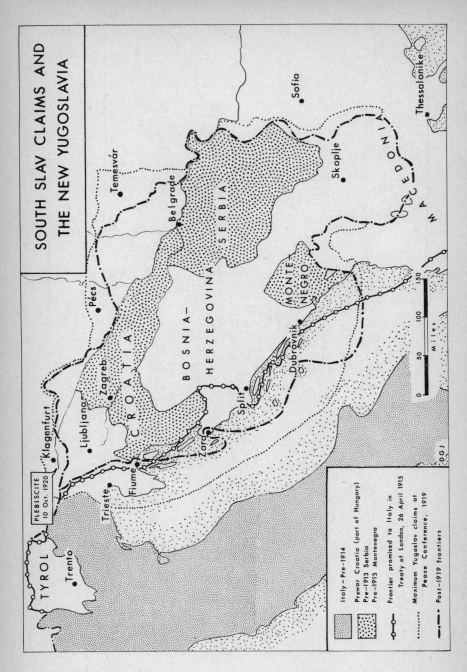

SOUTH SLAV CLAIMS AND
THE NEW YUGOSLAVIA

PLEBISCITE
10 Oct. 1920

TYROL

Trento

Trieste

Fiume

Klagenfurt

Ljubljana

Zagreb

C R O A T I A

Pécs

Temesvár

Belgrade

S E R B I A

Sofia

Thessaloníke

Skopje

M A C E D O N I A

MONTE-
NEGRO

Dubrovnik

Split

Zara

B O S N I A —
H E R Z E G O V I N A

Miles
0   50   100   150

Italy – Pre-1914

Prewar Croatia (part of Hungary)

Pre-1913 Serbia
Pre-1913 Montenegro

Frontier promised to Italy in
Treaty of London, 26 April 1915

Maximum Yugoslav claims at
Peace Conference, 1919

Post-1919 frontiers

D G J

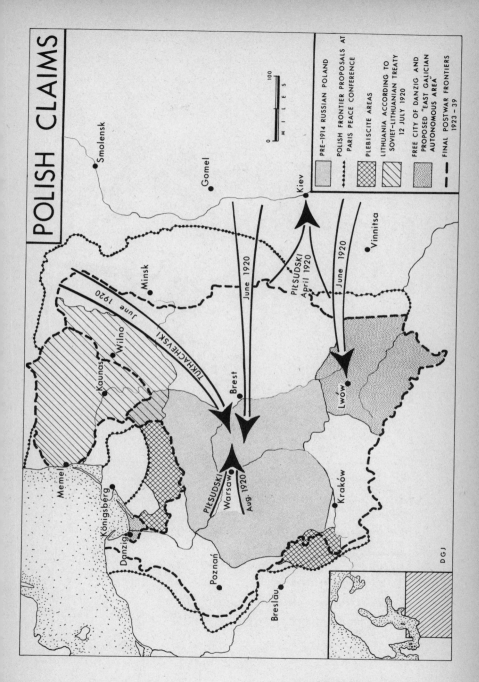

POLISH CLAIMS

Smolensk

Gomel

Kiev

Vinnitsa

PIŁSUDSKI
April 1920

June 1920

June 1920

Minsk

TUKHACHEVSKI June 1920

June 1920

Wilno

Kaunas

Brest

Lwów

Memel

Königsberg

PIŁSUDSKI
Warsaw Aug. 1920

Kraków

Danzig

Poznań

Breslau

PRE-1914 RUSSIAN POLAND

POLISH FRONTIER PROPOSALS AT
PARIS PEACE CONFERENCE

PLEBISCITE AREAS

LITHUANIA ACCORDING TO
SOVIET-LITHUANIAN TREATY
12 JULY 1920

FREE CITY OF DANZIG AND
PROPOSED "EAST GALICIAN
AUTONOMOUS AREA"

FINAL POSTWAR FRONTIERS
1923 - 39

100

M I L E S

0

DGJ

MAP 86   /169

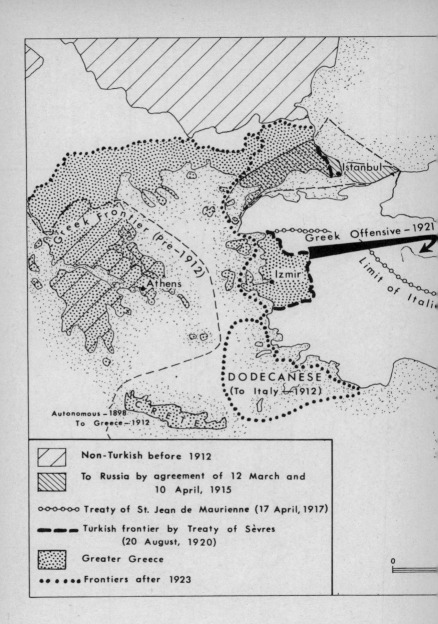

Istanbul

Greek Offensive – 1921

Limit of Italia

Izmir

Greek Frontier (pre-1912)

Athens

DODECANESE
(To Italy – 1912)

CRETE

Autonomous – 1898
To Greece – 1912

Non-Turkish before 1912

To Russia by agreement of 12 March and
10 April, 1915

Treaty of St. Jean de Maurienne (17 April, 1917)

Turkish frontier by Treaty of Sèvres
(20 August, 1920)

Greater Greece

Frontiers after 1923

0

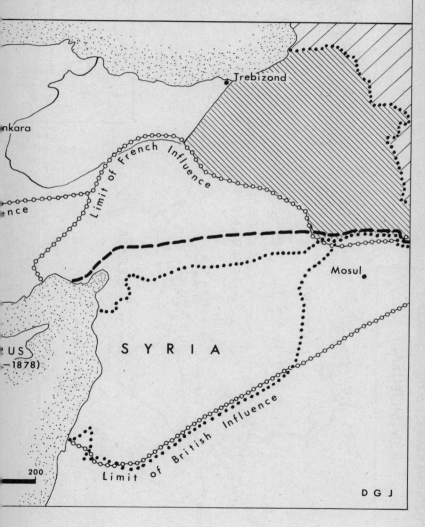

HE PARTITION OF TURKEY

Trebizond

nkara

Limit of French Influence

ence

Mosul

US
—1878)

S Y R I A

Limit of British Influence

200

D G J

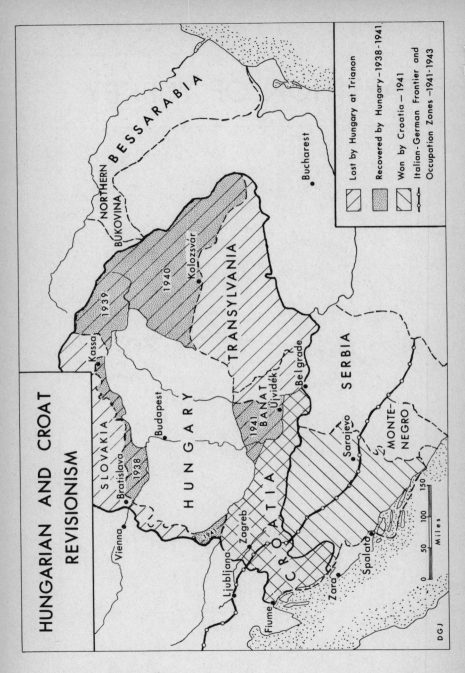

HUNGARIAN AND CROAT REVISIONISM

Lost by Hungary at Trianon

Recovered by Hungary – 1938 - 1941

Won by Croatia – 1941

Italian - German Frontier and Occupation Zones – 1941 - 1943

BESSARABIA

NORTHERN BUKOVINA

Bucharest

TRANSYLVANIA

Kolozsvár

1940

1939

Kassa

SLOVAKIA

Bratislava

1938

Vienna

Budapest

HUNGARY

SERBIA

Belgrade

Újvidék

BANAT

1941

MONTE-NEGRO

Sarajevo

Zagreb

CROATIA

1941

Ljubljana

Fiume

Zara

Spalato

Miles

0   50   100   150

DGJ

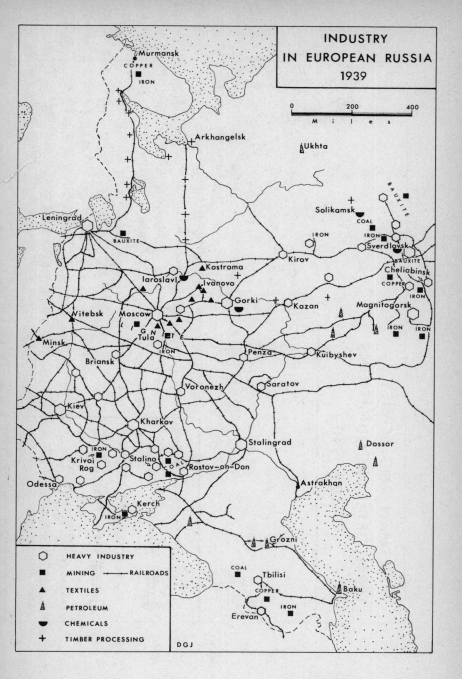

INDUSTRY
IN EUROPEAN RUSSIA
1939

0   200   400

M i l e s

Murmansk
COPPER
IRON

Arkhangelsk

Ukhta

Solikamsk
BAUXITE
COAL
IRON
IRON

Leningrad
BAUXITE

Sverdlovsk
BAUXITE

Kostroma
Iaroslavl
Ivanovo
Kirov

Cheliabinsk
COPPER
IRON

Gorki
Kazan

Magnitogorsk
IRON
IRON

Witebsk
Moscow
Tula
G N I T E
IRON

Penza
Kuibyshev

Minsk

Briansk

Voronezh
Saratov

Kiev

Kharkov

Dossor

Krivoi
Rog
IRON

Stalino
C O A L
Rostov-on-Don

Stalingrad

Odessa

Astrakhan

Kerch
IRON

Grozni

COAL
Tbilisi

COPPER
Baku

Erevan
IRON

Legend

- ⬡ HEAVY INDUSTRY
- ■ MINING   ——— RAILROADS
- ▲ TEXTILES
- ⌁ PETROLEUM
- ◖ CHEMICALS
- + TIMBER PROCESSING

D G J

MAP 89   /173

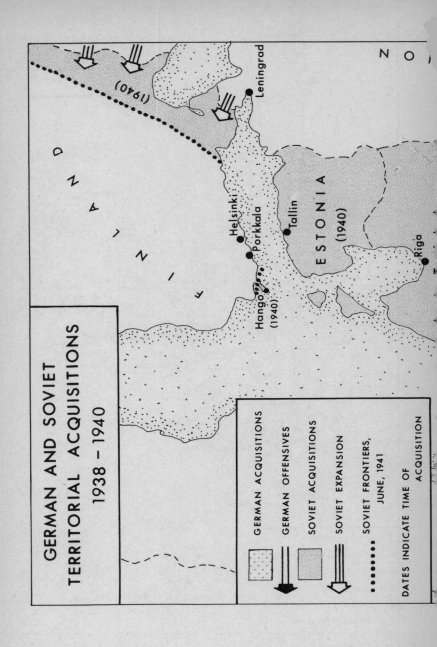

GERMAN AND SOVIET
TERRITORIAL ACQUISITIONS
1938 – 1940

Leningrad

Helsinki
Porkkala
Tallin
ESTONIA
(1940)
Riga

Hango
(1940)

F I N L A N D

(1940)

GERMAN ACQUISITIONS

GERMAN OFFENSIVES

SOVIET ACQUISITIONS

SOVIET EXPANSION

SOVIET FRONTIERS,
JUNE, 1941

DATES INDICATE TIME OF
ACQUISITION

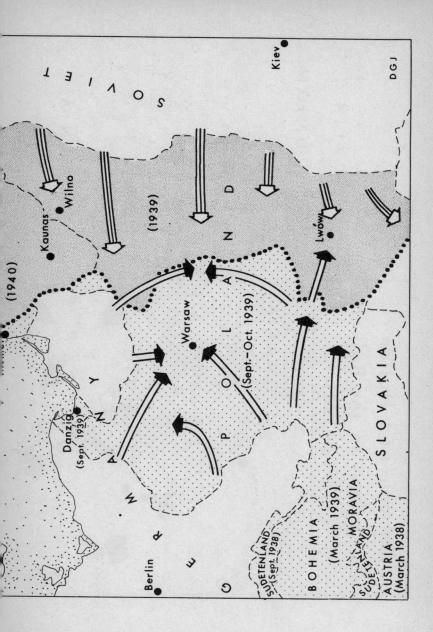

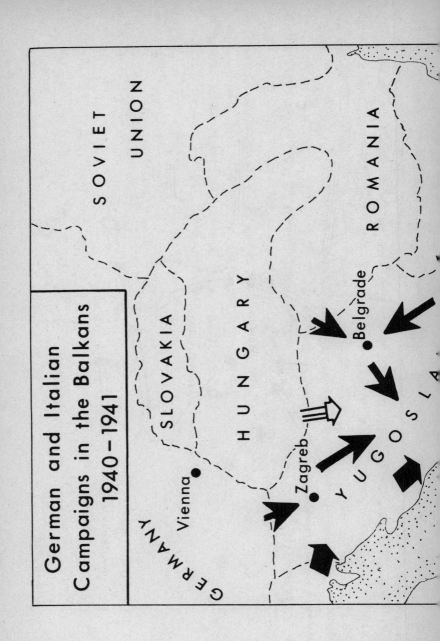

German and Italian
Campaigns in the Balkans
1940–1941

SOVIET UNION

SLOVAKIA

GERMANY

Vienna

HUNGARY

ROMANIA

Zagreb

Belgrade

YUGOSLA

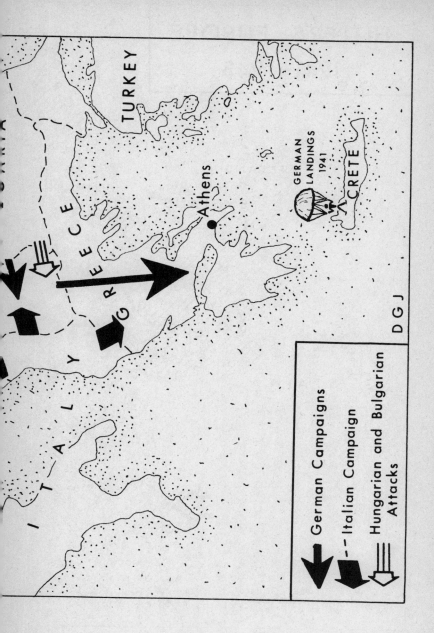

TURKEY

Athens

GERMAN
LANDINGS
1941

CRETE

ITALY

GREECE

DGJ

German Campaigns

Italian Campaign

Hungarian and Bulgarian
Attacks

HITLER'S EUROPE
1941–1943

IRELAND

ENGLAND

NORWAY

SWEDE

DENMARK

GERMANY

SLO

HU

VICHY
FRANCE

ITALY

CROATIA

PORTUGAL

SPAIN

0   200   400
M i l e s

DGJ

FINLAND

S O V I E T

U N I O N

Leningrad

Moscow

Minsk

w

Kiev

Stalingrad

Rostov

OMANIA

GARIA

T U R K E Y

•••••• Pre–Hitler Germany

Hitler's Germany

Allied
Advances:
Mid–1943

Hitler's Active Allies

Ruled by German Occupation
Forces: Mid–1943

Maximum Extent of German
Advance: 1941 and 1942

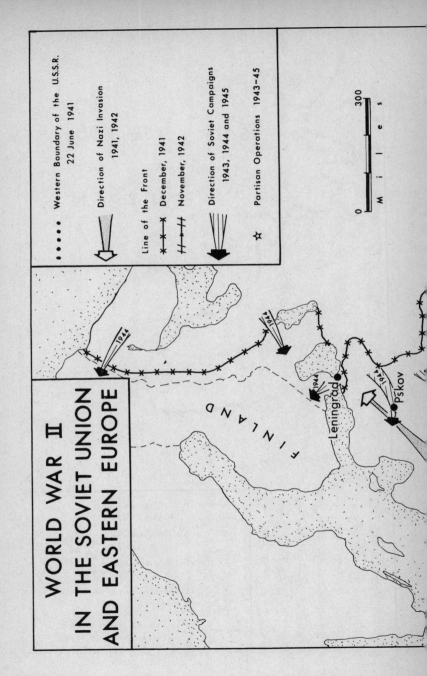

WORLD WAR II
IN THE SOVIET UNION
AND EASTERN EUROPE

Western Boundary of the U.S.S.R.
22 June 1941

Direction of Nazi Invasion
1941, 1942

Line of the Front

December, 1941

November, 1942

Direction of Soviet Campaigns
1943, 1944 and 1945

☆ Partisan Operations 1943–45

0 300

Miles

FINLAND

Leningrad

Pskov

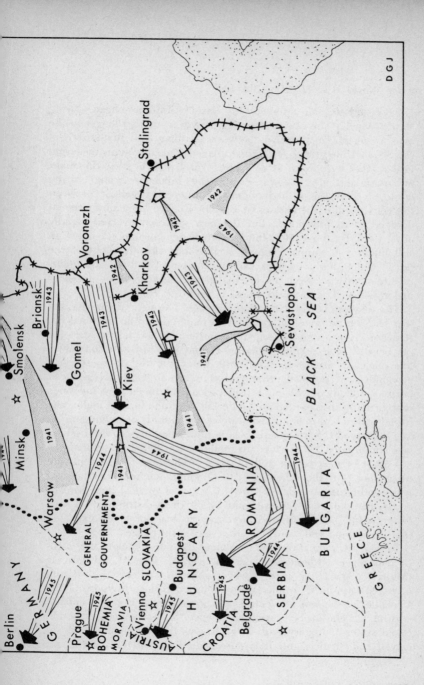

After World War II (MAPS 94–101)

A second era of autonomy in Eastern Europe began during World War II. The center of power, however, was no longer in the West or in the small nations between Germany and Russia, but in the Soviet Union (*Map 99*), which played a major role in defeating Hitler. This state, born after World War I, had become dominant in Eurasia and, after the war, exercised its influence throughout the world. Just as Russia had undergone temporary eclipse between the wars, so now the nations of Eastern Europe for a time seemed doomed to insignificance. But the new situation evolved rapidly after 1945. By the 1960's, the Eastern European nations, although still under Communist regimes established with the help of the Soviet Union, had won back varying degrees of cultural and political autonomy and were playing major roles in Soviet-bloc decision-making as well as in world affairs (*Maps 100, 101*).

The new era began under bad auspices. Throughout Eurasia, the war had left an appalling heritage of material and institutional destruction. Russia and Yugoslavia, for example, had lost at least ten per cent of their populations, and Poland had lost almost twenty-five per cent. Moreover, faced with the imperative to re-establish economic and political order and to settle millions of displaced persons, the men who made the peace had to employ measures that brutally disregarded the suffering of individuals. Finally, the former Allies had diametrically opposed standards of judgment. On one side stood the Americans, whose understanding of world affairs was conditioned by the fact that their nation had been spared the holocaust of destruction and by their dedication to constitutional democracy. On the other side stood Stalin, whose understanding was conditioned by almost three decades of cynical and bureaucratic manipulation of power and by his deep distrust of Western "imperialists." Given these differences, it was not to be expected that mere good will would create a successful peace.

In general, radical territorial changes did not dominate the negotiations for a settlement in Eastern Europe after World War II (*Maps 95–98*). There were, however, shifts in territory. With hardly an exception, the victorious Allies abolished Hitler's revisions of the Versailles settlement in Central and Southeastern Europe: Poland, Austria, Czechoslovakia, Yugoslavia, and Albania re-emerged as national states; Hungary and Bulgaria gave up what they had received from Hitler; and Italy surrendered not only Dalmatia and

Albania, but most of Istria and the Dodecanese Islands (*Map 96*). The Allies also recognized, in general, the revisions of the 1939–41 period of the Soviet Union's western frontier (*Map 94*): the Baltic states of Latvia, Lithuania, and Estonia remained in Soviet hands; Moscow's claim to a long strip of land possessed before the war by Finland, Poland, and Romania was accepted; and part of East Prussia as well as several pieces of Japan's Pacific empire were assigned to the Soviet Union. The Allies tolerated a most drastic change in eastern Germany. In compensation for its losses in the east, Poland was given half of East Prussia and all of Pomerania and Silesia up to the Oder and Neisse rivers (*Maps 95, 98*).

One of the most important of the new frontiers created in 1945–47 emerged more or less informally from a wartime agreement. This was the line between the Soviet and Western zones of occupation in Germany, which, in 1949, became the border between the western Federal Republic of Germany and the eastern German Democratic Republic (*Map 95*). The Allies also left permanently unsettled several of the most burning of the territorial issues that faced them. This was particularly true of the Oder-Neisse question and of Berlin, situated deep in the Soviet zone of Germany but occupied by Soviet, British, French, and United States forces (*Map 97*). The principal reason for such failures was that, even before the Peace Conference opened at Paris in 1946, political conflicts had completely overshadowed the territorial issues as the bases of international relationships.

Two factors combined to doom the prospects of peace after 1945. These were Western confusion about the causes of world-wide social and economic change, and the Soviet Union's abuse of its military power in occupied lands. In Europe, the coincidence between popular desires for change and the presence of the "Socialist" Red Army created optimum conditions for the seizure of power by the "leftist" (extremist) Communist elements in the European socialist movements, which, since 1919, had been instruments of the Soviet state. Where he could, Stalin apparently attempted to moderate revolutionary proclivities. But on the one hand, in several countries, strong-minded Communist leaders—such as the Yugoslav, Joseph Broz (Tito) (1945–19   ), pressed for radical socialist revolution; on the other hand, in Poland and elsewhere, where Stalin had specific war aims, native Communist groups were supported, and Soviet armies openly helped local Communists. Observing these events, Americans abandoned their belief that Stalin's intentions were peaceful and concluded that Soviet Communism was at last beginning the world conquest its ideological prophets had long foretold. In 1946, the United States undertook to resist Communist expansion in Greece and to isolate Stalin's power in Germany. In 1947, Stalin replied to an American effort to aid Europe's reconstruction (the Marshall Plan) by announcing that the world was now divided into "two camps." The Cold War followed.

By 1950, a Soviet military bloc had been established that included virtually all of Eastern Europe as well as Communist China (*Map 101*). The only nations not included were Finland, Greece (which remained under Western influence at the cost of a ruinous civil war), and Yugoslavia (which had been expelled from the Communist camp in 1948 because its leaders were more interested in building a Communist system in Yugoslavia than in being subservient to Stalin). Until 1953, when Stalin died, the fundamental problems of Eastern Europe and the Soviet Union were shunted aside while the Communist bloc engaged in massive industrialization and the Korean War (1950–53).

After Stalin's death, the Communist world evolved until each of the member states had gained some degree of national autonomy and some influence in decision-making. Because of the tensions inherited from Stalin's terroristic centralism, and because of the continuing Cold War, progress was uneven. In 1955 and 1956, several Soviet acts suggested that Stalinism was a thing of the past. Soviet troops evacuated Austria. Nikita Khrushchev (1955–64) sought reconciliation with Tito and, at the Twentieth Party Congress of the CPSU (1956), ruthlessly attacked Stalin's ways. These evidences of relaxation excited new hopes in Eastern Europe. Polish nationalist unrest and worker disturbances in the summer of 1956 created a crisis that local Communists used to win enough freedom from the Soviet Union to begin following a Polish "road to socialism." In Budapest, a popular outburst of sympathy for the Poles sparked a serious revolt. The policies of the Hungarian Communist Party had been too harsh, and Soviet domination of Hungary had been too heavy-handed. Only Soviet military intervention prevented Hungary's withdrawal from the bloc.

As a consequence of the struggle between Moscow and Peking for leadership of the international Communist movement, Soviet–Eastern European relationships changed decisively after 1958. One East European state, Albania, sided with the Chinese. In order to prevent others from following this example, the Soviet leaders were compelled to tolerate the further growth of political autonomy among the other members of the bloc. Like Yugoslavia, Poland and Romania in 1966 could be classified as "national Communist states," although unlike Yugoslavia their foreign policies were still dictated by Soviet interests. Hungary, East Germany, and Czechoslovakia in the 1960's were eagerly suggesting further changes to the Soviet Union.

Eastern Europe and the Soviet Union still suffered many ills in 1966. It was to be doubted that the bloc would have held together except for the continuing threat of Soviet military intervention. Yet, in the second half of the twentieth century, Russia and Eastern Europe appeared to be solving many of the old political, economic, and cultural problems. To many peoples around the world who had rejected Western political hegemony, the examples set by these nations seemed promising models for study and imitation.

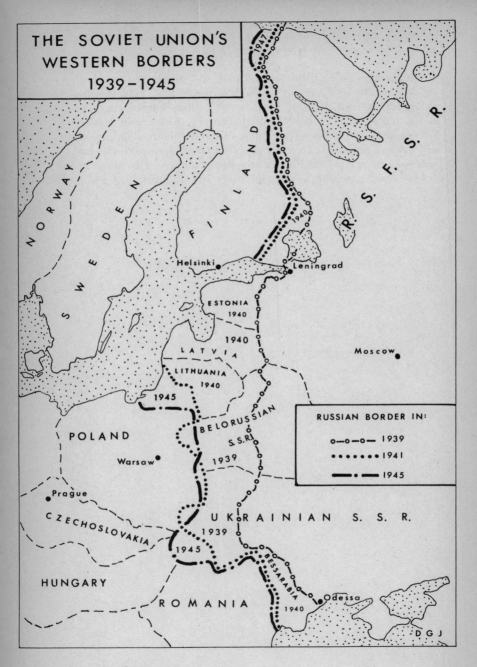

THE SOVIET UNION'S WESTERN BORDERS 1939–1945

NORWAY

SWEDEN

FINLAND

R. S. F. S. R.

1947

Helsinki

Leningrad

1940

ESTONIA
1940

Moscow

1940

LATVIA

LITHUANIA
1940

1945

BELORUSSIAN
S.S.R.

POLAND

Warsaw

1939

RUSSIAN BORDER IN:

o—o—o 1939
• • • • • • 1941
•—•—• 1945

Prague

CZECHOSLOVAKIA

1939
1945

UKRAINIAN S. S. R.

HUNGARY

BESSARABIA

Odessa

ROMANIA

1940

D G J

DIVIDED GERMANY AND AUSTRIA

NETHERLANDS

BRITISH ZONE

Hamburg

Rostock

SOVIET

ZONE

Hannover

Berlin

POLAND

Dortmund

G
E
R
M
A
N
Y

Leipzig

Bonn

BELG.

Chemnitz

FRENCH ZONE

Frankfurt

LUX.

Saarbrücken

U.S. ZONE

CZECHOSLOVAKIA

FRANCE

Stuttgart

FRENCH

Freiburg

Munich

U.S.

Salzburg

SOVIET

Vienna

AUSTRIA

HUNGARY

SWITZERLAND

FRENCH

BRITISH

Graz

ITALY

YUGOSLAVIA

MAP 95   /187

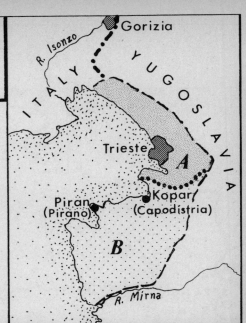

FREE TERRITORY OF TRIESTE 1947

- –·–·– Italian–Yugoslav border
- ········· Boundary of Free Territory of Trieste
- **A** British–American Occupation Zone
- **B** Yugoslav Occupation Zone

R. Isonzo

Gorizia

ITALY

YUGOSLAVIA

Trieste

A

Piran (Pirano)

Kopar (Capodistria)

B

R. Mirna

GERMANY

EAST GERMANY

FRENCH SECTOR

WEST

EAST

BRITISH SECTOR

Brandenburger Tor

SOVIET SECTOR

BERLIN

U.S. SECTOR

BERLIN

DIVIDED BERLIN 1945

DGJ

The Polish Problem

1939 to the Present

Baltic Sea

Riga

L A T V I A

LITHUANIA

Kaliningrad

Vilnius

Gdansk

E A S T   P R U S S I A

Szczecin

Białystok

U. S. S. R.

Brest

Pinsk

Warsaw

GERMANY

Szklarska
Poręba

Wrocław

Kraków

Lvov

Boundaries:
●●●●Curzon
Line
—·—1939
▨▨▨1945 to present
Annexed:
to Russia – 1939
from Germany – 1945

DGJ

0   100
M i l e s

MAP 98   */189*

SOVIET UN

LENINGRAD

Vorkuta
Coal

Lithuanian S.S.R.
Latvian S.S.R.
Estonian S.S.R.

Belorussian S.S.R.

Ukrainian S.S.R.

Moldavian S.S.R.

CENTRAL
Cherepovets

Moscow
INDUSTRIAL
REGION

Russian S

DONBASS

Kursk

VOLGA REGION

URAL REGION

Georgian S.S.R.

Armenian S.S.R.

Azerbaijan S.S.R.

K a z a k h

Karaganda

S. S. R.

Uzbek S.S.R.

Turkmen S.S.R.

Kirgiz S.S.R.

Tajik S.S.R.

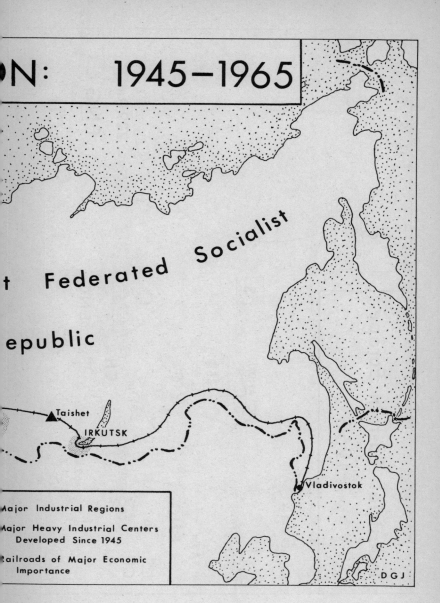

t Federated Socialist

epublic

▲Taishet

IRKUTSK

Vladivostok

Major Industrial Regions

Major Heavy Industrial Centers
   Developed Since 1945

Railroads of Major Economic
   Importance

DGJ

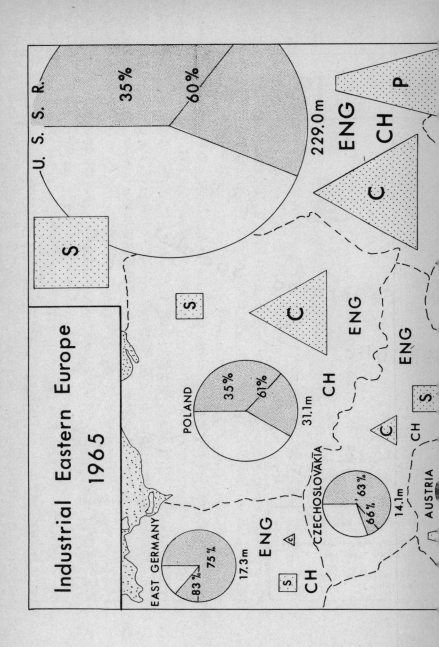

Industrial Eastern Europe 1965

U. S. S. R.

35%

60%

229.0 m

S

ENG

CH

C

P

S

C

ENG

CH

ENG

S

POLAND

35%

61%

31.1m

C

CH

CH

S

CZECHOSLOVAKIA

63%

66%

14.1m

AUSTRIA

EAST GERMANY

83%

75%

17.3m

ENG

S

CH

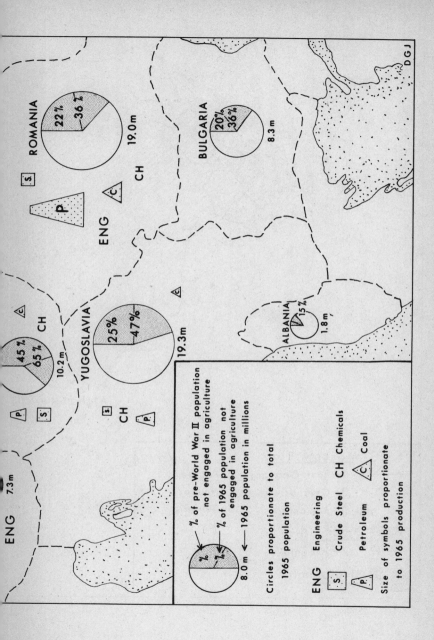

ENG   7.3m

ROMANIA

22%
36%

S

P

ENG   CH   19.0m

C

BULGARIA

20%
36%

8.3m

45%
65%
10.2m

P   CH   C

S

YUGOSLAVIA

25%
47%

CH   19.3m

S

P

C

ALBANIA
15%
1.8m

% of pre-World War II population
  not engaged in agriculture

% of 1965 population not
  engaged in agriculture

8.0 m — 1965 population in millions

%
T

Circles proportionate to total
1965 population

ENG   Engineering

S   Crude Steel   CH   Chemicals

P   Petroleum   C   Coal

Size of symbols proportionate
to 1965 production

DGJ

193

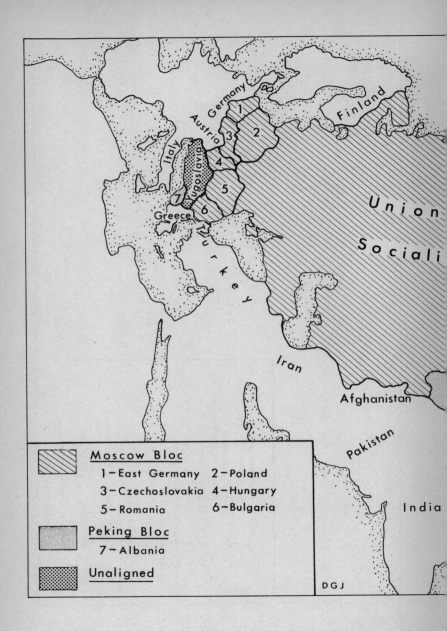

Moscow Bloc
1 – East Germany   2 – Poland
3 – Czechoslovakia   4 – Hungary
5 – Romania   6 – Bulgaria

Peking Bloc
7 – Albania

Unaligned

DGJ

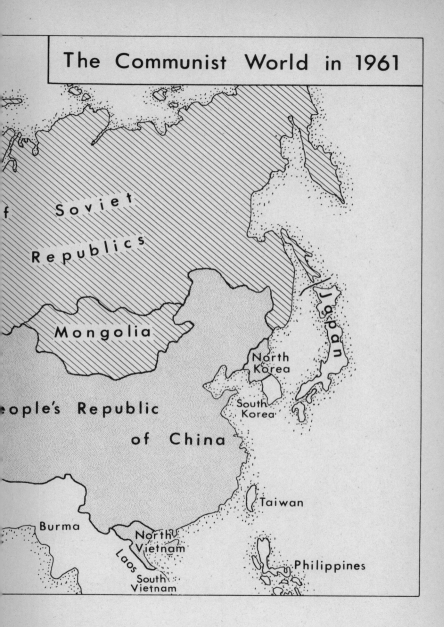

The Communist World in 1961

Soviet Republics

Mongolia

eople's Republic of China

Japan

North Korea

South Korea

Burma

North Vietnam

Laos

South Vietnam

Taiwan

Philippines

Sources

Atlas S.S.S.R. (*Atlas of the U.S.S.R.*). Moscow, 1960.

BAVILOV, S. I. (editor-in-chief). *Bolshaia sevetskaia entsiklopediia* (*The Great Soviet Encyclopedia*). 51 vols. 2d ed.; Moscow, 1948–58. With annual supplements, 1957–63.

BAZICHEVICHA, K. U. (general editor). *Atlas istorii SSSR dlia srednie shkoly* (*Historical Atlas of the U.S.S.R. for Secondary Schools*). 3 vols. Moscow, 1959.

BUKHARIN, N. I., KUIBYSHEV, V. V., and M. N. POKROVSKII (editors). *Bolshaia sovetskaia entsiklopediia* (*The Great Soviet Encyclopedia*). 65 vols. Moscow, 1926–31. With supplement, *Soiuz sovetskikh sotsialisticheskikh respublik* (*Union of Soviet Socialist Republics*). Moscow, 1947.

The Cambridge Medieval History. 8 vols. Cambridge and New York, 1911–36. Map Supplements.

The Cambridge Modern History. Vol. XIV. *Atlas.* Cambridge and New York, 1924.

DVORNIK, FRANCIS. *The Slavs in European History and Civilization.* New Brunswick, N.J., 1962.

GLAVNOE UPRAVLENIE GEODEZII I KARTOGRAFII MINISTERSTVA GEOLOGII OKHRANY NEDR SSSR (CHIEF ADMINISTRATION OF GEODESY AND CARTOGRAPHY OF THE U.S.S.R. MINISTRY OF GEOLOGY AND CARE OF RESOURCES). *Atlas SSSR* (*Atlas of the U.S.S.R.*). Moscow, 1962.

HÓMAN, BÁLINT and GYULA SZEKFÜ. *Magyar Történet* (*History of Hungary*). 5 vols. Budapest, 1935–38.

KOSMINSKII, E. A. and A. P. LEVANDOVSKII. *Atlas istorii srednikh vekov* (*Historical Atlas of the Middle Ages*). 2d ed.; Moscow, 1958.

Magyarország Története: Egyetemi Tankönyv' (*Hungarian History: University Textbook*). Budapest, 1960–65.

MAKKAI, LÁSZLÓ. *Histoire de la Transylvanie* (*History of Transylvania*). Paris, 1946.

MANTEUFFEL, TADEUSZ (editor). *Historia Polski* (*History of Poland*). Warsaw, 1957–60.

MARKERT, WERNER (general editor). *Osteuropa Handbuch: Jugoslawien* (*East European Handbook: Yugoslavia*). Cologne, 1954.

———. *Osteuropa Handbuch: Polen* (*East European Handbook: Poland*). Cologne, 1959.

Novyi entsiklopedicheskii slovar (*The New Encyclopedic Dictionary*). 82 vols. Moscow, 1890–1907. With supplement.

OSTROGORSKY, GEORGE. *History of the Byzantine State*. Oxford, 1956.

PALMER, R. R. (editor). *Historical Atlas of the World*. New York, 1961.

SHEPHERD, WILLIAM R. *Historical Atlas*. 8th ed.; New York, 1956.

STADTMÜLLER, GEORG. *Geschichte Sudosteuropas* (*History of Southeastern Europe*). Munich, 1956.

TRETIAKOV, P. N. (editor). *Istoriia Bolgarii* (*History of Bulgaria*). Moscow, 1954.

ZEISSIG, HANS (editor). *Neuer Geschichts- und Kulturatlas* (*New Historical and Cultural Atlas*). Frankfurt-am-Main, 1950.

Index

Bold face numbers following entries refer to map numbers.